COLORADO TRAILS

NORTH-CENTRAL REGION

Warning: While every effort has been made to make the trail descriptions in this book as accurate as possible, some discrepancies may exist between the text and the actual trail. Hazards may have changed since the research and publication of this edition. Adler Publishing Company, Inc., and the authors accept no responsibility for the safety of users of this guide. Individuals are liable for all costs incurred if rescue is necessary.

Printed in the United States of America.

Cover photos
Clockwise from bottom left: Middle Fork of the Swan Trail, Boreas Pass Trail, Red Cone Peak Trail

Rear cover photos
From left: Mount Bross Trail, Mosquito Pass Trail

COLORADO TRAILS
NORTH-CENTRAL REGION

PETER MASSEY
JEANNE WILSON

ADLER
PUBLISHING

Acknowledgements
We would like to express gratitude to the staff at the U.S. Forest Service, the Denver Public Library, the Colorado Historical Society, and the various Chambers of Commerce throughout Colorado who have given us guidance in our research.

We would like to recognize especially the following for their major contributions to this endeavor:

Cover Design Concept: **Rudy Ramos**
Text Design and Maps: **Deborah Rust Design**
Copyediting: **Alice Levine**
Proofreading: **James Barnett**

Adler Publishing Company, Inc.
1601 Pacific Coast Highway, Suite 290
Hermosa Beach, CA 90254
Toll-free: 800-660-5107
Fax: 310-698-0709
4WDbooks.com

Contents

Using This Book

Route Planning

The regional map on page 16 provides an overview of the trails in this book. Each 4WD trail is highlighted, as are the major highways and towns, which makes it possible to relate the start and end points of every 4WD trail in this book to nearby roads and trails.

By referring to the map you can plan your overall route to utilize as many 4WD trails as possible. Checking the difficulty rating and time required for each trail allows you to finalize your plans.

Difficulty Ratings

We utilize a point system to indicate the difficulty of each trail. Any such system is subjective and is dependent on the driver's experience level and the current road conditions.

We have rated the 4WD trails in this book on a scale of 1 to 10, 1 being passable for a normal passenger vehicle in good conditions and 10 requiring a heavily modified vehicle and an experienced driver who is willing to expect vehicle damage. Because this book is designed for owners of unmodified 4WD vehicles whom we assume do not want to risk damage to their vehicles, nearly all the trails are rated 5 or lower.

This is not to say that all the trails in this book are easy. We strongly recommend that inexperienced drivers not tackle any 4- or 5-rated trails before undertaking a number of the lower-rated ones, so that they can gauge their skill level and prepare for the difficulty of the higher-rated trails.

In assessing the trails, we assume good road conditions (dry road surface, good visi-bility, and so on). Our ratings are based on the following factors:

- obstacles such as rocks, mud, ruts, and stream crossings
- the stability of the road surface
- the width of the road and the vehicle clearance between trees or rocks
- the steepness of the road
- the margin of error (for example, a very high, open shelf road would be rated more difficult even if it was not very steep and had a stable surface)

The following is a guide to the ratings. As a rule only one of the criteria need to be met for the road to get a higher rating:

Rating 1: Graded dirt but suitable for a normal passenger vehicle. Gentle grades; fairly wide; very shallow water crossings (if any).

Rating 2: Road surface rarely or not maintained. Dirt road better suited to a high-clearance vehicle but passable in a normal passenger car; fairly wide, passing not a concern; mud not a concern under normal weather conditions.

Rating 3: High-clearance 4WD preferred. Rough road surface to be expected; mud possible but easily passable; rocks up to six inches in diameter; loose surface possible; shelf road but wide enough for passing or with adequate pull-offs.

Rating 4: High-clearance 4WD recommended. Rough road surface with rocks larger than six inches possible, but a reasonable driving line available; mud possible but passable; stream crossings less than fifteen inches deep; substantial sections of single-lane shelf road possible; moderate grades; moderately loose surface possible.

Rating 5: High-clearance 4WD required. Rough, rutted surface; rocks up to nine inches possible; mud may be impassable for inexperienced drivers; stream crossings up to twenty-four inches deep; sections may be steep enough to cause traction problems; very narrow shelf road with steep drop-offs should be expected; tight clearance between rocks or trees possible.

Rating 6: Experienced four-wheel drivers only. Potentially dangerous; large rocks, ruts, or terraces may need to be negotiated; steep slopes, loose surface, and/or very narrow vehicle clearance; stream crossings at least twenty-four inches deep, and/or unstable stream bottom, or difficult access; very narrow shelf road with steep drop-offs and challenging road surfaces to be expected.

Rating 7: Skilled, experienced four-wheel drivers only. Very challenging sections; very steep sections likely; loose surface, large rocks, deep ruts, and tight clearance expected; mud likely to necessitate winching.

Rating 8 to 10: Stock vehicles are likely to be damaged and may find the trail impassable. Well beyond the scope of this book.

Scenic Ratings

If rating the degree of difficulty is subjective, rating scenic beauty is guaranteed to lead to arguments—especially in Colorado, a stunningly beautiful state. However, we have tried to give some guide to the relative scenic quality of the various trails. The ratings are based on a scale of 1 to 10, with 10 being the most scenic.

Estimated Driving Times

In calculating driving times, we have not allowed for stops. Actual driving time may be considerably longer than indicated, depending on the number and duration of stops. Add more time if you prefer to drive more slowly than good conditions allow.

As with the distance cited for each trail, the time given for trails that dead-end is for travel one-way. The time that should be allowed for the overall trip, including the return to the start, may be as much as dou-

ble that indicated. However, with the knowledge of the trail that has been gained going in, you may find that the return is usually completed more quickly.

Current Road Conditions

All the 4WD trails described in this book may be impassable in poor weather conditions. For each trail, we have provided a phone number for obtaining current information about conditions.

Abbreviations

The route directions provided for the 4WD trails in this book use a series of abbreviations.

SO	Continue straight on
TL	Turn left
TR	Turn right
BL	Bear left
BR	Bear right
UT	U-turn

Using Route Directions

To help you stay on track, we have described and pinpointed (by odometer reading) nearly every significant feature along the route (intersections, streams, gates, cattle guards, and so on) and have provided directions to follow from these landmarks. Odometer readings will vary from vehicle to vehicle, but you will soon learn to allow for slight variations.

If you diverge from the route, zero your trip meter upon your return and continue the route, making the necessary adjustment to the point-to-point odometer directions. We have regularly reset the odometer readings in the directions, so you won't have to recalculate for too long. Route directions include cross-references whenever the route crosses another 4WD trail included in this book, which allows easy change of route or destination. Directions for traveling the 4WD trails in reverse are printed in blue. When traveling in reverse, read from the bottom of the table and work up.

Latitude and longitude readings are provided periodically to facilitate the use of a

Global Positioning System (GPS) receiver. These readings may also assist in finding your location on your maps. The GPS coordinates were taken using the NAD 1927 datum and are in the format dd°mm.mmm'. When loading coordinates into your GPS receiver, you may wish to include only one decimal place because in Colorado, the third decimal place equals only about two yards and the second less than twenty yards.

Map References

We recommend that you supplement the information in this book with more-detailed maps. Each trail in this book refers to various sheet maps and road atlases that provide the detail necessary to navigate and identify accurately your location. Typically, the following five references are given:

■ U.S. Forest Service Maps—Scale 1:126,720

■ U.S. Geological Survey County Series Maps—Scale 1:50,000

■ *The Roads of Colorado,* 1st ed. (Fredericksburg, Texas: Shearer Publishing, 1996)—Scale 1:158,400

■ *Colorado Atlas & Gazetteer,* 2nd ed. (Freeport, Maine: DeLorme Mapping, 1995)—Scale 1:160,000 and 1:320,000

■ *Trails Illustrated* topo maps; National Geographic maps—Various scales, but all contain good detail

We recommend the *Trails Illustrated* maps. They are reliable, easy to read, and printed on nearly indestructible plastic "paper." However, the series does not cover all the 4WD trails described in this book.

If *Trails Illustrated* maps are not available, we recommend the U.S. Geological Survey County Series Maps. These show the necessary detail without being too detailed. Their main weakness is that some are out of date and do not show the 4WD trails accurately.

The two atlases are reasonably priced and include maps of the entire state. Although the atlases do not give much information for each 4WD trail beyond what we have provided, they are helpful if you wish to explore side roads. Of the two,

we prefer *The Roads of Colorado.*

U.S. Forest Service maps lack the detail of the other sheet maps and, in our experience, are also out of date occasionally. They have the advantage of covering a broad area. These maps are most useful for the longer trails.

For those who want to navigate with the assistance of a portable computer, Maptech publishes a particularly good series of maps on CD ROM. These are based on the U.S. Geological Survey 7.5° Series Maps—Scale 1:24,000, but they can be viewed on four scales. The 1:100,000-scale series are also included. These maps offer many advantages over normal maps:

■ GPS coordinates for any location can be found, which can then be loaded into your GPS receiver. Conversely, if you know your GPS coordinates, your location on the map can be pinpointed instantly.

■ Towns, rivers, passes, mountains, and many other sites are indexed by name so that they can be located quickly.

■ 4WD trails can be marked and profiled for elevation change and distance from point to point.

■ Customized maps can be printed out.

To cover the entire state of Colorado requires 8 CD ROMs, which is expensive; however, the CD ROMs can be purchased individually.

All these maps should be available through good map stores. The CD ROMs are available directly from Maptech (800-627-7236 or on the Internet at www.maptech.com).

Driving Off-Highway

Four-wheel driving involves special road rules and techniques. This section is provided as an introduction for 4WD beginners.

4WD Road Rules

To help ensure that these trails remain open and available for all four-wheel drivers to enjoy, it is important to minimize your impact on the environment and not be a safety risk to yourself or anyone else. Remember that the 4WD clubs in Colorado fight a constant battle with the U.S. Forest Service to retain access.

The fundamental rule when traversing the 4WD trails described in this book is to use common sense. In addition, special road rules for 4WD trails apply.

■ Vehicles traveling uphill have the right of way.

■ If you are moving more slowly than the vehicle behind you, pull over to let the other vehicle by.

■ Park out of the way in a safe place. Set the parking brake—don't rely on leaving the transmission in park. Manual transmissions should be left in the lowest gear.

In addition to these rules, we offer the following advice to four-wheel drivers.

■ Size up the situation in advance.

■ Be careful. Take your time.

■ Maintain smooth, steady power and momentum.

■ Engage 4WD and low-range before you get into a tight situation.

■ Steer toward high spots and try to put the wheel over large rocks.

■ Straddle ruts.

■ Use gears rather than only the brakes to hold the vehicle when driving downhill. On very steep slopes, chock the wheels when you park your vehicle.

■ Watch for logging and mining trucks.

■ Wear your seat belt and ensure that all luggage, especially heavy items such as tool boxes or coolers, is secured. Heavy items should be secured by ratchet tie-down straps rather than elastic-type straps, which are not strong enough to hold heavy items if the vehicle rolls.

Tread Lightly!

Remember the rules of the Tread Lightly!® program.

■ Become informed. Obtain maps, regulations, and other information from the U.S. Forest Service or from other public land agencies. Learn the rules and follow them.

■ Resist the urge to pioneer a new road or trail or to cut across a switchback. Stay on constructed tracks and avoid running over young trees, shrubs, and grasses, damaging or killing them. Don't drive across alpine tundra; this fragile environment may take years to recover.

■ Stay off soft, wet roads and 4WD trails readily torn up by vehicles. Repairing the damage is expensive.

■ Travel around meadows, steep hillsides, stream banks, and lake shores that are easily scarred by churning wheels.

■ Stay away from wild animals that are rearing young or suffering from a food shortage.

■ Obey gate closures and regulatory signs.

■ Preserve America's heritage by not disturbing old mining camps, ghost towns, or other historical features.

■ Carry out all rubbish.

■ Stay out of designated wilderness areas. They are closed to all vehicles. Know where the boundaries are.

■ Get permission to cross private land. Leave livestock alone. Respect landowners' rights.

Special Four-Wheel Driving Techniques

Certain obstacles are likely to be encountered on Colorado's 4WD trails. The following provides an introduction to the techniques required for dealing with the most common situations.

Rocks. Tire selection is important because sharp rocks are often encountered on Colorado mountain 4WD trails. Select a multiple-ply, tough sidewall, light-truck tire with a large-lug tread.

As you approach a rocky stretch, get into 4WD low range to give you maximum slow-speed control. Speed is rarely necessary since traction on a rocky surface is usually good. Plan ahead and select the line you wish to take. If the rock appears to be larger than the clearance of your vehicle, don't try to straddle it. Check to see that it is not higher than the frame of your vehicle once you get a wheel over it. Put a wheel up to the rock and slowly climb it; then gently drop over the other side, using the brake to ensure a smooth landing. Bouncing the car over rocks increases the likelihood of damage, as the body's clearance is reduced by the suspension compressing. Running boards also significantly reduce your clearance in this respect.

Steep Uphill Grades. Consider walking the trail to ensure that it is passable, especially if it is clear that backtracking is going to be a problem.

Select 4WD low range to ensure that you have adequate power to pull up the hill. If the wheels begin to lose traction, try turning the steering wheel gently from side to side to give the wheels a chance to regain traction.

If you lose momentum, but the car is not in danger of sliding, use the foot brake, switch off the ignition, leave the vehicle in gear (if manual transmission) or park (if automatic), engage the parking brake, and get out to examine the situation. See if you can remove any obstacles, and figure out the line you need to take. Reversing a couple of yards and starting again may allow you to get better traction and momentum.

If you decide a stretch of road is impassably steep, back down the trail. Trying to turn the vehicle around is extremely dangerous and very likely to cause it to roll over.

Steep Downhill Grades. Again, consider walking the trail to ensure that it is passable, especially if it is clear that backtracking is going to be a problem.

Select 4WD low range, in first gear, to maximize braking assistance from the engine. If the surface is loose and you are losing traction, change up to second or third gear. Do not use the brakes if you can avoid it, but don't let the vehicle's speed get out of control. Feather (lightly pump) the brakes if you slip under braking.

Travel very slowly over rock ledges or ruts. Attempt to tackle these diagonally, letting one wheel down at a time.

If the vehicle begins to slide around at the back, gently apply the throttle and correct the steering. If the rear of the vehicle starts to slide sideways, do not apply the brakes.

Mud. Muddy trails are easily damaged, so they should be avoided if possible. If you do need to traverse a section of mud, your success will depend heavily on whether you have open-lugged mud tires or chains. Thick mud fills the tighter tread that is on normal tires, leaving the tire with no more grip than if it were bald. If the muddy stretch is only a few yards long, the momentum of your vehicle may allow you to get through regardless.

If the muddy track is very steep, either uphill or downhill, do not attempt it. Your vehicle is very likely to skid in such conditions and the vehicle may roll or slip off the edge of the road.

When crossing mud:

■ Avoid making detours off existing tracks, so that environmental damage is minimized.

■ Check to see that the mud has a reasonably firm base (tackling deep mud is definitely not recommended unless you have a vehicle-mounted winch—and even then, be cautious because the winch may not get you out).

■ Check to see that no ruts are too deep for the ground clearance of your vehicle.

Having decided that you can get through and having selected the best route, use the following techniques:

■ Select 4WD low range and a suitable gear; momentum is the key to success, so use a high enough gear to build up sufficient speed.

■ Avoid accelerating heavily, so as to minimize wheel spinning and provide maximum traction.

■ Follow existing wheel ruts, unless they are too deep for the clearance of your vehicle.

■ Correct slides by turning the steering wheel in the direction that the rear wheels are skidding, but don't be too aggressive with the amount you correct your steering.

■ If the vehicle comes to a stop, don't continue to accelerate, as you will only spin your wheels and dig yourself into a rut. Try backing out and having another go.

Stream Crossings. By crossing a stream that is too deep, drivers risk far more than water flowing in and ruining the interior of their vehicles. Water sucked into the engine's air intake will seriously damage the engine. Likewise, water that seeps into the air vent on the transmission or differential will mix with the lubricant and may lead to serious problems. Water that gets into the interior of modern vehicles may damage the computerized vehicle management system. Even worse than damage to a vehicle is the possibility that deep or fast flowing water could easily carry a vehicle downstream and may endanger the lives of the occupants.

The manual for some 4WDs will say what fording depth the vehicle can negotiate safely. If your vehicle's owner's manual doesn't include this information, your local dealer may be able to assist. If you don't know, then you should try to avoid crossing through water that is more than a foot or so deep.

The first rule for crossing a stream is to know what you are getting into. You need to ascertain how deep the water is, make sure that there are no large rocks or holes and that the bottom is solid enough to avoid getting the vehicle bogged, and see that the entry and exit points are negotiable. This assessment may take some time and you may get wet, but to cross a stream without first properly evaluating the situation is to take a great risk.

The secret to water crossings is to keep moving, but not to move too quickly. In shallow water (where the surface of the water is below the bumper), your primary concern is to safely negotiate the bottom of the stream, avoiding any rock damage and maintaining momentum if there is a danger of getting stuck or slipping on the exit.

In deeper water (between eighteen and thirty inches deep), the objective is to create a small bow wave in front of the moving vehicle. This requires a speed that is approximately walking pace. The bow wave reduces the depth of the water around the engine compartment. If the water's surface reaches your tailpipe, select a gear that will maintain moderate engine revs to avoid water backing up into the exhaust; do not change gears midstream.

Crossing water deeper than thirty inches requires more extensive preparation of the vehicle and should be attempted only by experienced drivers.

Snow. The trails in this book are nearly all closed until the snow has melted or been bulldozed. Therefore, the only snow conditions that you are likely to encounter are an occasional snowdrift that has not yet melted or fresh snow from an unexpected storm. Getting through such conditions depends on the depth of the snow, its consistency, the stability of the underlying surface, and your vehicle.

If the snow is no deeper than about nine inches and there is solid ground beneath it, it should not pose a problem. In deeper snow that seems solid enough to support your vehicle, be extremely cautious: If you break through a drift, you are likely to be stuck, and if conditions are bad, you may have a long wait.

The tires you use for off-highway driving, with a wide tread pattern, are probably suitable for these snow conditions. Nonetheless, it is wise to carry chains (preferably for all four wheels) and even wiser to travel with a vehicle-mounted winch.

It is important to remember how quickly the weather can change in the Colorado high country, even in summer. Pack clothes and other items to ensure your survival if you are caught in a sudden storm.

Sand. As with most off-highway situations, your tires will affect your ability to cross sand. It is difficult to tell how well a particular tire will handle in sand just by looking at it, so be guided by the manufacturer and your dealer.

The key to driving in soft sand is floatation, which is achieved by a combination of low tire pressure and momentum. Before crossing a stretch of sand, you should start by reducing your tire pressure to between fifteen and twenty pounds. If necessary, you can safely go to as low as twelve pounds. As you cross the sand, maintain momentum so that your vehicle rides on the top of soft sand without digging in or stalling. This may require plenty of engine power.

Air the tires back up as soon as you are out of the sand to avoid damage to the tires and the rims. Airing back up requires a high-quality air compressor. Even then, it is a slow process.

The only trail in this book that may

necessitate lowering the tire pressure for sand is the Medano Pass road, which ends in the Great Sand Dunes National Monument. A refill station at the national monument is open in the peak season, which may mean that if you air down on this trail, you can avoid buying a portable compressor.

Vehicle Recovery Methods

You are sure to get stuck sooner or later. The following techniques will help you get back going. The most suitable method will depend on the equipment available and the situation you are in—whether you are stuck in sand, mud, or snow, or high-centered, or unable to negotiate a hill.

Towing. Use a strong nylon yank strap, twenty to thirty feet long, two to three inches wide, rated to at least 20,000 pounds, and preferably with looped ends. This type of strap will stretch 15 to 25 percent, and the elasticity will assist in extracting the vehicle.

Attach the strap to a frame-mounted tow hook. Ensure that the driver of the stuck vehicle is ready, take up all but about six feet of slack, and then move the towing vehicle away at a moderate speed (in most circumstances this means using 4WD low range in second gear) so that the elasticity of the strap is employed in the way it is meant to be. Don't take off like a bat out of hell or you risk breaking the strap or damaging a vehicle.

Never join two yank straps together with a shackle. If one strap breaks, the shackle will become a lethal missile aimed at one of the vehicles (and anyone inside). For the same reason, never attach a yank strap to the tow ball on either vehicle.

Jacking. Jacking the vehicle may allow you to pack under the wheel (with rocks, dirt, or logs) or use your shovel to remove an obstacle. However, the standard vehicle jack is unlikely to be of as much assistance as a high-lift jack. We highly recommend purchasing a good high-lift jack as a basic accessory if you decide that you are going to do a lot of serious, off-highway, four-wheel driving.

Tire Chains. Tire chains can be of assistance in mud and snow. Link-type chains provide much more grip than cable-type chains. There are also dedicated mud chains with larger, heavier links than normal snow chains.

It is best to have chains fitted on all four wheels. However, this may not be possible since some vehicles lack sufficient clearance between the wheel and the fender. Remove chains from the front wheels as soon as practicable to avoid undue strain on the vehicle.

Be aware that it is more difficult to fit the chains after you are stuck; if at all possible try to predict their need and have them on the vehicle before trouble arises.

Winching. Most people using this book will not have a winch. But if you get serious about four-wheel driving, this is probably the first major accessory you will consider buying.

Under normal circumstances, a winch would be warranted only for the more difficult 4WD trails in this book. Having a winch is certainly comforting when you see a difficult section of road ahead and have to decide whether to risk it or turn back. Major obstacles can appear when you least expect them, even on trails that are otherwise easy.

A winch is not a panacea to all your recovery problems. Winching depends on the availability of a good anchor point, and an electric winch may not work if it is submerged in a stream. Despite these constraints, no accessory is more useful than a high-quality, powerful winch when you get into a difficult situation.

If you acquire a winch, learn to use it properly; take the time to study your owner's manual. Incorrect operation can be extremely dangerous and may cause damage to the winch or to trees, which are the most common anchors.

Navigation by the Global Positioning System (GPS)

Although this book is designed so that each trail can be navigated by simply following the detailed directions provided, nothing makes navigation easier than a GPS receiver.

The Global Positioning System (GPS)

consists of a network of twenty-four satellites, nearly thirteen thousand miles in space, in six different orbital paths. The satellites are constantly moving, making two complete orbits around the earth every twenty-four hours at about 8,500 miles per hour. Each satellite is constantly transmitting data, including its identification number, its operational health, and the date and time. It also transmits its location and the location of every other satellite in the network.

By comparing the time a signal was transmitted to the time it is received, a GPS receiver calculates how far away each satellite is. With a sufficient number of signals, the receiver can then triangulate its location. With three or more satellites, the receiver can determine latitude and longitude coordinates. With four or more, it can calculate altitude. By constantly making these calculations, it can calculate speed and direction.

The U.S. military uses the system to provide positions accurate to within half an inch. However, civilian receivers are less sophisticated and are deliberately fed slightly erroneous information in order to effectively deny military applications to hostile countries or terrorists. Because of this degradation of the signal, which is called Selective Availability (SA), the common civilian receivers have an accuracy of twenty to seventy-five yards.

A GPS receiver offers the four-wheel driver numerous benefits.

■ You can track to any point for which you know the longitude and latitude coordinates with no chance of heading in the wrong direction or getting lost. Most receivers provide an extremely easy-to-understand graphic display to keep you on track.

■ It works in all weather conditions.

■ It automatically records your route for easy backtracking.

■ You can record and name any location, so that you can relocate it with ease. This may include your campsite, a fishing spot, or even a silver mine you discover!

■ It displays your position, allowing you to pinpoint your location on a map.

■ By interfacing the GPS receiver directly to a portable computer, you can monitor and record your location as you travel (using the appropriate map software) or print the route you took.

GPS receivers have come down in price considerably in the past few years and are rapidly becoming indispensable navigational tools. Many higher-priced cars now offer integrated GPS receivers; and within the next few years, receivers will become available on most models.

Battery-powered, hand-held units that meet the needs of off-highway driving currently range from less than $100 to a little over $300 and continue to come down in price. Some high-end units feature maps that are incorporated in the display, either from a built-in database or from interchangeable memory cards. However, none of these maps currently include 4WD trails in their database.

If you are considering purchasing a GPS unit, look for the following features:

■ Price. The very cheapest units are likely outdated and very limited in their display features. Expect to pay $125 to $300.

■ The number of channels, which means the number of satellites that the unit tracks concurrently. Many older units have only one channel that switches from one satellite to another to collect the required information. Modern units have up to twelve channels, which are each dedicated to tracking one satellite. A greater number of channels provides greater accuracy, faster start-up (because the unit can acquire the initial data it needs much more rapidly), and better reception under difficult conditions (for example, if you are in a deep canyon or in dense foliage).

■ The number of routes and the number of sites (or "waypoints") per route that can be stored in memory. For off-highway use, it is important to be able to store many waypoints so that you do not have to load coordinates into the machine as frequently. Having sufficient memory also ensures that you can automatically store your location without fear that you will run out of memory.

■ It is also important that the machine can store numerous routes. GPS receivers enable you to combine waypoints to form a route, greatly simplifying navigation. As you reach each waypoint, the machine automatically swaps to the next one and directs you there.

■ The better units store up to five hundred waypoints and twenty reversible routes of up to thirty waypoints each. Also consider the number of characters a GPS receiver allows you to use in naming waypoints. When you try to recall a waypoint, you may have difficulty recognizing names restricted to only a few characters.

■ Automatic route storing. Most units automatically store your route as you go along and enable you to display it in reverse to make backtracking easy.

■ The display. Compare graphic displays. Some are much easier to decipher or offer more alternative displays.

■ The controls. Because GPS receivers have many functions, they need to have good, simple controls.

■ Vehicle mounting. To be useful, the unit needs to be located so that it can be read easily by both the driver and the navigator. Check that the unit can be conveniently located in your vehicle. Units have different shapes and mounting systems.

■ Position-format options. Maps use different grids; you should be able to display the same format on your GPS unit as on the map you are using, so that cross-referencing is simplified. There are a number of formats for latitude and longitude, as well as the UTM (Universal Transverse Mercator) grid, which is used on some maps.

After you have selected a unit, a number of optional extras are also worth considering:

■ A cigarette lighter adapter. Important because GPS units eat batteries!

■ A vehicle-mounted antenna, which will improve reception under difficult conditions. (The GPS unit can only "see" though the windows of your vehicle; it cannot monitor satellites through a metal roof.) Having a vehicle-mounted antenna also means that you do not have to consider reception when locating the receiver in your vehicle.

■ An in-car mounting system. If you are going to do a lot of touring using the GPS, you may want to attach a bracket on the dash rather than relying on a velcro mount.

■ A computer-link cable. Data from your receiver can be downloaded to your PC; or, if you have a laptop computer, you can monitor your route as you go along, using one of a number of inexpensive map software products on the market.

We used a Garmin 45 receiver to take the GPS positions in this book. This unit is now outdated, but it has served us well for the past five years in our travels throughout the United States and around the world.

Trails in the North-Central Region

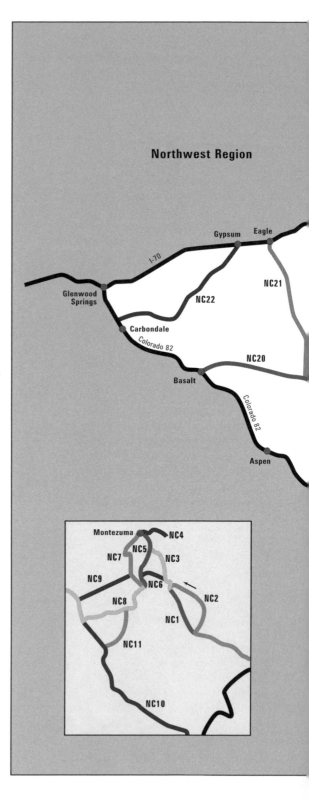

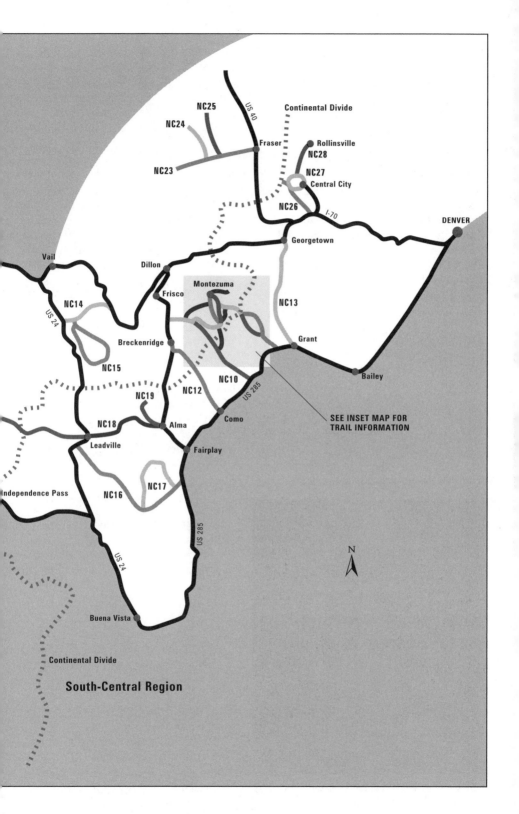

NC25

NC24

NC23

Continental Divide

US 40

Fraser

Rollinsville

NC28

NC27

Central City

NC26

I-70

DENVER

Georgetown

Vail

Dillon

Montezuma

Frisco

NC13

NC14

US 24

Grant

Breckenridge

NC15

Bailey

NC19

NC12

NC10

US 285

SEE INSET MAP FOR
TRAIL INFORMATION

NC18

Alma

Como

Leadville

Fairplay

Independence Pass

NC16

NC17

US 285

N

Buena Vista

US 24

Continental Divide

South-Central Region

Handcart Gulch Trail

STARTING POINT Intersection of US 285 and Park County 60 (FR 120) at the town site of Webster

FINISHING POINT Webster Pass

TOTAL MILEAGE 9.6 miles

UNPAVED MILEAGE 9.6 miles

DRIVING TIME 1 3/4 hours

ROUTE ELEVATION 9,200 feet to 12,096 feet

USUALLY OPEN Mid-August to late September

DIFFICULTY RATING 5

SCENIC RATING 9

Special Attractions

■ Varied four-wheel driving challenges, including an extremely narrow shelf road.
■ Spectacular views, particularly of Red Cone Peak.
■ Access to an extensive network of 4WD trails.

History

The area is named for two prospectors who in 1860 brought their handcart loaded with supplies up the valley and made the area's first gold discovery while panning the creek.

Lower section of Handcart Gulch Trail

Towns that developed in the vicinity included Webster, Hall Valley, and Handcart Gulch. Webster was a staging point for passengers and freight headed across Webster Pass. For a time in the 1870s it was the end of the line for the Denver, South Park & Pacific Railroad. It was known as a wild town where gunplay was common; traffic was heavy to the boot hill cemetery north of town. As the railroad was extended and better pass routes were opened, Webster went into decline. Its post office closed in 1909.

The town of Hall Valley, also known as Hall's Gulch, Hallville, and Hall City, was centered on the fortunes of the Whale Mine. At the town's peak, around 1876–1877, the population reached about 500. Hall Valley was renowned as a very rowdy place where the saloons were open all day and all night. When two of the mine foremen who had earned the wrath of the miners for their bullying management were in town, the miners lynched them both!

It is not clear if Col. J. W. Hall was the owner or the manager of the Whale Mine, but it is clear that both he and the English company that operated it subsequently were incompetent, and as the fortunes of the mine declined, so did the town.

The town of Handcart Gulch, located a short distance farther up the valley, was also short-lived and its prosperity mirrored that of Hall Valley.

Description

The route starts at the town site of Webster (nothing remains of the town) at the intersection of US 285 and Park County 60 (FR 120), 3.2 miles west of Grant.

Initially, this is the same route that leads to Webster Pass by way of Red Cone Peak. The well-maintained 2WD road travels along Hall Valley beside the headwaters of the North Fork of the South Platte River though pine and aspen groves.

After the intersection with Red Cone Peak Trail five miles along the route, the road soon becomes rough and rocky. Large rocks in the road make selecting the correct line

The narrow shelf section of Handcart Gulch Trail descending from Webster Pass before switchbacking into the valley

important. There is a very muddy and wheel-rutted spot just in front of a log cabin 1.7 miles after the turnoff to Red Cone. With permission from the cabin's owner, you can bypass the muddy stretch by driving through the yard.

The road continues through two manageable creek crossings and then commences its final assault on the pass. The ascent begins with a number of switchbacks and culminates in a long, very narrow, off-camber rough shelf cut into the steep talus mountainside. This stretch of road is frequently obstructed by rocks that you must clear in order to pass; it is only just wide enough for a full-sized vehicle to squeeze through. The last hundred feet are usually blocked by a snowdrift until late into summer.

The view from the pass is wonderful: To the east is the one-way (downhill only) road off Red Cone Peak, southeast is the west face of Red Cone, north is the Snake River Valley, and southwest is the shelf road you have just ascended.

Current Road Conditions

Pike National Forest
South Platte Ranger District
19316 Goddard Ranch Court
Morrison, CO 80465
(303) 275-5610

Map References

USFS Pike NF
USGS Summit County #2
      Park County #1
      Park County #2
Trails Illustrated, #104 (route incomplete)
The Roads of Colorado, p. 71
Colorado Atlas & Gazetteer, pp. 38, 48–49

Route Directions

▼ 0.0	From intersection of US 285 and Park County 60 (FR 120) at the site of Webster, zero trip meter. Proceed west on unpaved road marked with sign to Red Cone Road and Handcart Gulch.
5.0 ▲	End at intersection with US 285 at the

site of Webster.

GPS: N 39°27.46' W 105°43.27'

▼ 0.9 SO Enter Pike National Forest.
4.1 ▲ SO Leave Pike National Forest.

▼ 1.7 SO Track on left with campsite. Cattle
guard.
3.3 ▲ SO Cattle guard. Track on right with campsite.

▼ 2.9 SO Burning Bear walking trail on right.
Town site of Hall Valley.
2.1 ▲ SO Burning Bear walking trail on left.
Town site of Hall Valley.

GPS: N 39°28.46' W 105°45.70'

▼ 3.1 SO Road on left to Beaver Creek (FR 123).
1.9 ▲ SO Road on right to Beaver Creek
(FR 123).

▼ 4.6 SO USFS Handcart Campground.
0.3 ▲ SO USFS Handcart Campground.

▼ 4.9 SO Hall Valley Campground and Gibson
Lake Trailhead (FR 120B) to the left.
Town site of Handcart Gulch.
0.1 ▲ SO Hall Valley Campground and Gibson
Lake Trailhead (FR 120B) to the right.
Town site of Handcart Gulch.

GPS: N 39°28.98' W 105°48.20'

▼ 5.0 TL T-intersection. Turn left onto road to
Handcart Gulch (FR 121). Track on
right is North-Central #2: Red Cone
Peak Trail, which also leads to Webster
Pass. Zero trip meter.
0.0 ▲ Proceed along Handcart Gulch road
(FR 120).

GPS: N 39°29.02' W 105°48.27'

▼ 0.0 Proceed along Handcart Gulch road.
4.6 ▲ BR Intersection. Left goes to North-Central
#2: Red Cone Peak and loops back to
Webster Pass. Right leads to US 285.
Zero trip meter.

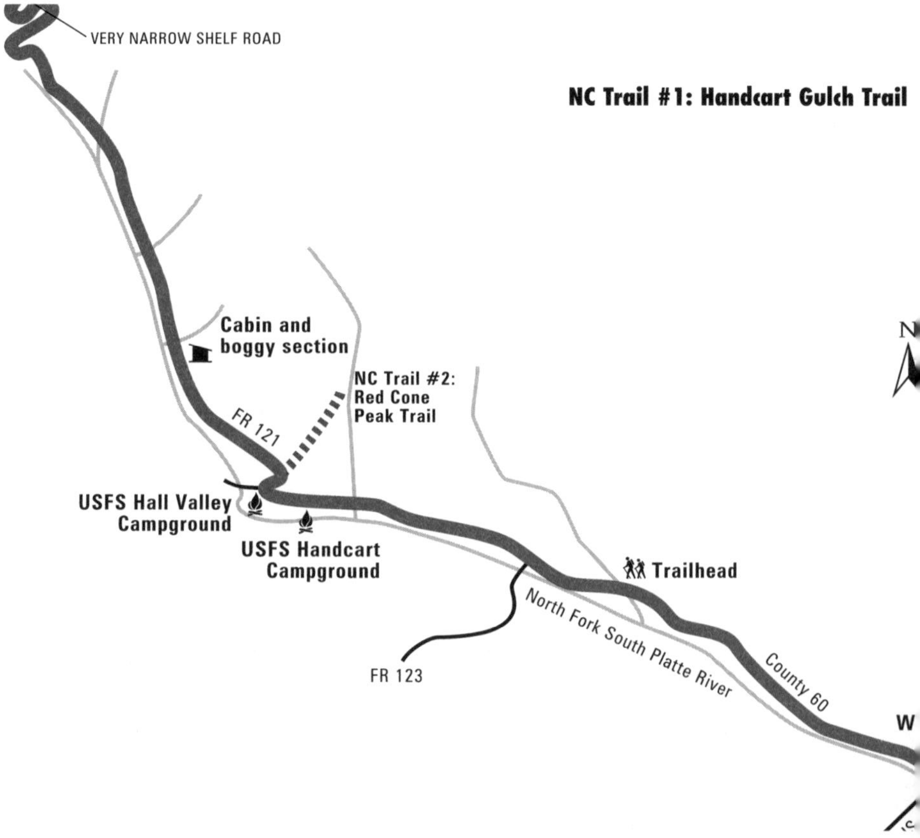

NC Trail #1: Handcart Gulch Trail

VERY NARROW SHELF ROAD

Cabin and
boggy section

NC Trail #2:
Red Cone
Peak Trail

FR 121

USFS Hall Valley
Campground

USFS Handcart
Campground

🚶 Trailhead

North Fork South Platte River

County 60

FR 123

$50,000 WAITING TO BE FOUND

Jim Reynolds was one of the first settlers in Fairplay, but when the Civil War started, he left to join the Confederate Army. Toward the end of the war, he and eight other soldiers, including his brother, returned to Colorado to steal gold to help fund the war effort.

They held up a stage in South Park and raced along the South Platte River with a posse hot on their tails. They eventually evaded their pursuers by crossing Webster Pass and making camp on Deer Creek, having hidden the loot on the way.

The posse finally caught up with them. One of Reynolds's gang was killed in the shoot-out, but the rest got away. The posse displayed the head of the unfortunate robber in Fairplay.

Jim Reynolds was eventually captured and put on trial in Denver, along with four others in the gang. All five were convicted and sentenced to jail in Fort Leavenworth. While being transported there, they were all shot and killed.

Reynolds revealed the location of the gold he had hidden, but no one has been able to find it. It is supposed to be buried in Handcart Gulch. Its value today would be $50,000.

▼ 0.1	SO	Track on right.
4.5 ▲	BR	Track on left.

▼ 0.4	BL	Intersection. FR 5652 on right.
4.1 ▲	BR	Intersection. FR 5652 on left.

▼ 0.5	SO	Track on right to walking trail.
4.0 ▲	SO	Track on left to walking trail.

▼ 1.7	SO	Building on right. Potentially very boggy and rutted section of the track.
2.9 ▲	SO	Building on left. Potentially very boggy and rutted section of the track.

▼ 2.8	SO	Cross through creek.
1.8 ▲	SO	Cross through creek.

▼ 3.1	SO	Cross through creek.
1.5 ▲	SO	Cross through creek.
		GPS: N 39°31.31' W 105°49.89'

▼ 4.2-4.6	SO	Travel along a very narrow shelf.
0.0-0.4 ▲	SO	Travel along a very narrow shelf.

▼ 4.6		End at Webster Pass.
0.0 ▲		From the summit of Webster Pass, zero trip meter and proceed south on Handcart Gulch road (FR 120) along a narrow shelf.
		GPS: N 39°31.86' W 105°49.92'

Red Cone Peak Trail

STARTING POINT Intersection of US 285 and Park County 60 (FR 120), at the town site of Webster
FINISHING POINT Webster Pass
TOTAL MILEAGE 11.2 miles
UNPAVED MILEAGE 11.2 miles
DRIVING TIME 2 hours
ROUTE ELEVATION 9,200 feet to 12,600 feet
USUALLY OPEN Early July to late September
DIFFICULTY RATING 7
SCENIC RATING 10

Special Attractions

- Spectacular alpine views.
- The adventure of tackling a very challenging 4WD trail.
- Access to an extensive network of 4WD trails.

Special Note on the Difficulty Rating of this Road

This trail is the most difficult included in this book. We have limited the scope of this book primarily to trails with difficulty ratings up to a maximum of 5. So why include one rated 7? First, the views are fabulous. Second, it provides a route for those four-

Looking across Hall Valley to Red Cone Peak Trail as it descends to Webster Pass (marked)

wheelers who want to test their skills on a truly demanding road. However, be warned. Some experienced four-wheel drivers consider this the most dangerous 4WD trail in the state.

The route offers a range of challenges. Clearance is very tight between the trees in the early part of the trail. There are also a number of very tight switchbacks, severely eroded sections, and quite large (and not always imbedded) rocks. However, these obstacles by themselves would warrant a difficulty rating of only 5.

By far the most challenging and potentially dangerous obstacle is the very steep downhill section of loose talus at the end of the trail. It is because of this section that the U.S. Forest Service has banned travel on this road from the Webster Pass direction, making the road one-way only. If you do not handle your vehicle properly when descending the talus slope, the rear of the vehicle is likely to swing around, causing it to roll. The

floor of Handcart Gulch is about 1,500 feet below-and that is where you will stop!

However, there is a safe way to make the descent: Select first gear in low range and go down slowly. You must exercise particular care if you use the brakes because if the wheels lock up, the rear of the vehicle will swing around. If the back of the vehicle starts to come around, the only way to straighten it is to accelerate. In the heat of a crisis, however, many drivers will find the need to accelerate the opposite of their instincts. If you need to employ this technique, be careful not to overdo it. This steeply descending section of road is bumpy because of broad corrugations caused by vehicles sliding on the talus; if you have to accelerate, be prepared to bounce all over the place.

Description

This trail commences at the intersection of North-Central #1: Handcart Gulch Trail, five miles from US 285. Navigating this trail is easy, as there are no other side roads.

The start of Red Cone Peak Trail is quite rocky. The road travels through pine and aspen forest that becomes just pine as the road ascends. The clearance between the trees is just wide enough for a full-sized vehicle. The road crosses a creek bed that is often heavily eroded. Along the way, you will also encounter a number of switchbacks and rocks. A couple of uphill sections (although short) are quite challenging because of large rocks and a loose, eroded surface.

After emerging from timberline, the road travels along a lengthy, open tundra ridge before making its final, sharp ascent to a narrow perch above the steep, dangerous descent to Webster Pass. This is a good place to stop and admire one of the most breathtaking views in Colorado while gathering yourself for the last section, now in clear view.

The distance from the summit of Red Cone Peak to Webster Pass is about three-quarters of a mile and is broken into three short, steep sections, with the first being the hardest.

From Webster Pass, you get to look back on the slope you have just negotiated and across to the vivid red surface of Red Cone Peak.

Heading down the steep section of the Red Cone Peak Trail

Current Road Conditions

Pike National Forest
South Platte Ranger District
19316 Goddard Ranch Court
Morrison, CO 80465
(303) 275-5610

Map References

USFS Pike NF
Trails Illustrated, #104 (route incomplete)
Colorado Atlas & Gazetteer, pp. 38, 48

Route Directions

▼ 0.0   From intersection of US 285 and Park County 60 (FR 120) at the site of Webster, zero trip meter. Proceed northwest on unpaved road marked with sign to Red Cone

Road and Handcart Gulch.
GPS: N 39°27.46′ W 105°43.27′

▼ 0.9 SO Enter Pike National Forest.
▼ 1.7 SO Track on left with campsite. Cattle guard.
▼ 2.9 SO Burning Bear walking trail on right.
▼ 3.1 SO Road on left to Beaver Creek (FR 123).
▼ 4.6 SO USFS Handcart Campground.
▼ 4.9 SO Hall Valley Campground and Gibson Lake Trailhead (FR 120B) to the left.
GPS: N 39°28.98′ W 105°48.20′

▼ 5.0 TR T-intersection. Road on left is North-Central #1: Handcart Gulch Trail (FR 121), which also leads to Webster Pass. Zero trip meter and proceed along Red Cone Peak Trail (FR 565).
GPS: N 39°29.02′ W 105°48.27′

NC Trail #2: Red Cone Peak Trail

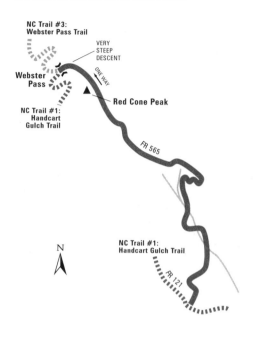

▼ 0.1 TR Sign for Webster Pass.
▼ 1.0 SO Cross through creek.
▼ 3.6 BL Fork in road.
▼ 5.5 SO First steep descent.
▼ 6.2   End at Webster Pass crossing.
       GPS: N 39°31.90′ W 105°49.92′

NORTH-CENTRAL REGION TRAIL #3

Webster Pass Trail

STARTING POINT Webster Pass, at the intersection of FR 285, North-Central #1: Handcart Gulch Trail (FR 121) and North-Central #2: Red Cone Peak Trail
FINISHING POINT Montezuma
TOTAL MILEAGE 4.9 miles
UNPAVED MILEAGE 4.9 miles
DRIVING TIME 1/2 hour
ROUTE ELEVATION 10,300 feet to 12,096 feet
USUALLY OPEN Early July to late September
DIFFICULTY RATING 3
SCENIC RATING 8

Special Attractions
■ Views from the summit.
■ Access to an extensive network of 4WD trails.
■ Attractive Snake River Valley.

History
Native Americans used Webster Pass for many years before the arrival of the white man. Prospectors first traveled the pass in the 1860s, and in 1878, a partnership of the Webster brothers and the Montezuma Silver Mining Company built a wagon road over the crossing. The route was the main freight route to the Snake River mining district. The itinerant Father Dyer traveled across the route regularly to deliver the mail and conduct his far-flung ministry. In the early 1890s, David Moffat, the president of the Denver & Rio Grande Railroad, surveyed the crossing at Webster Pass as a possible rail route. The road fell into disuse and was reopened in 1971 through the efforts of 4WD clubs.

Description
This route takes you from Webster Pass, where it intersects the roads over Red Cone Peak and through Handcart Gulch, down the Snake River Valley and into the township of Montezuma. From the pass, there is a magnificent view of the Handcart Gulch area to the southeast and the Snake River Valley to the northwest. The road up Red Cone Peak is one way and cannot be entered from Webster Pass. A snowdrift usually blocks the alternative road into Handcart Gulch until late in summer.

The route remains above timberline as it switchbacks down from Webster Pass on a reasonably wide road that has a sound surface. Passing other vehicles is easy at the switchbacks. As you reach the valley floor, you will cross the headwaters of the Snake River and pass the road toward Radical Hill, which departs to the left.

This route is simple to navigate.

Current Road Conditions
Pike National Forest
South Platte Ranger District

Mountain goats grazing at Webster Pass

9316 Goddard Ranch Court
Morrison, CO 80465
(303) 275-5610

Map References

USFS White River NF
USGS Summit County #2
      Park County #1
Trails Illustrated, #104
The Roads of Colorado, p. 71 (Webster Pass
Road incorrectly shown as FR 215)
Colorado Atlas & Gazetteer, p. 38

Route Directions

▼ 0.0   From the summit of Webster Pass, zero
        trip meter and proceed down FR 285.
3.9 ▲   End at intersection with North-Central
        #2: Red Cone Peak Trail straight ahead
        (a one-way road with no entry from
        this point) and North-Central #1:
        Handcart Gulch Trail to the right.
        GPS: N 39°31.90' W 105°49.92'

▼ 1.4   SO Cross Snake River. Track to the left is
        North-Central #6: Radical Hill Trail.
2.5 ▲   SO Track to the right is North-Central #6:
        Radical Hill Trail. Cross Snake River.
        GPS: N 39°32.27' W 105°50.44'

▼ 2.6   SO Cross through creek, then intersection.

        Campsites on right. Remnants of old
        building. Track on left closed off.
1.3 ▲   SO Track on right closed off. Remnants of
        old building. Campsites on left.
        Intersection. Then cross through creek.

▼ 3.2   SO Seasonal closure gate.
0.7 ▲   SO Seasonal closure gate.

▼ 3.3-3.8 SO Tracks on right and left.
0.1-0.6 ▲ SO Tracks on right and left.

▼ 3.9   TR Intersection of Webster Pass Trail and
        North-Central #5: Deer Creek Trail
        (County 5/FR 5). Zero trip meter.
0.0 ▲   Proceed along Webster Pass Trail
        (FR 285).
        GPS: N 39°34.10' W 105°51.57'

▼ 0.0   Proceed north along County 5.
1.0 ▲   TL Intersection of North-Central #5: Deer
        Creek Trail (County 5/FR 5) and

NC Trail #3: Webster Pass Trail

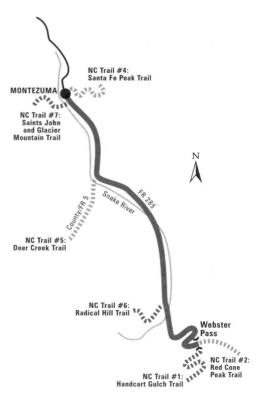

Webster Pass Trail switchbacking up to the intersection with Red Cone Peak at the pass

		Webster Pass Road. Zero trip meter.
▼ 0.3	SO	Ruins of mine and log buildings.
0.7 ▲	SO	Ruins of mine and log buildings.
▼ 1.0		End at Montezuma Snake River Fire Station.
0.0 ▲		From the Montezuma Snake River Fire Station, zero trip meter and proceed south on County 5 (FR 5).
		GPS: N 39°34.85′ W 105°52.03′

NORTH-CENTRAL REGION TRAIL #4

Santa Fe Peak Trail

STARTING POINT Montezuma

FINISHING POINT Santa Fe Peak near the Silver Wave Mine, at the end of a dead-end road (FR 264)

TOTAL MILEAGE 5.2 miles

UNPAVED MILEAGE 5.2 miles

DRIVING TIME 1 1/2 hours (one-way)

ROUTE ELEVATION 10,300 feet to 12,800 feet

USUALLY OPEN Early June to early October

DIFFICULTY RATING 5

SCENIC RATING 9

Special Attractions
- Spectacular, panoramic alpine views.
- Shelf road with some very challenging sections.
- Many other 4WD trails in the vicinity.

Description
This route commences at the first intersection on the left as you drive into Montezuma from Keystone (or, coming from the fire station, the last intersection on the right). The unpaved route heads uphill through the homes within the town limits. At this point there are a number of side roads, but stay on the main road and proceed up a series of mild switchbacks. As the road ascends from timberline, it begins a tighter series of switchbacks.

Once you are out of town, navigation becomes fairly straightforward. The road levels out as it travels along an open ridge which provides some wonderful views. It then commences another series of short switchbacks before leveling off at an open, rocky meadow that offers spectacular 360-degree views.

As you leave this meadow, the road becomes significantly more difficult—especially if you are in a full-sized vehicle. It narrows, becomes rougher, and has a loose surface. As you proceed, the road starts to descend gently around a rocky, narrow shelf with a steep drop-off along the west side of Santa Fe Peak. We recommend that from this point you park your vehicle in an out-of-the way spot and walk down to the Silver Wave Mine, as there is no place to turn around at the mine. You may park along a ridge just under half a mile from the mine or at the last switchback, about 150 yards before the mine. The ridge provides a great view of Geneva Creek Valley to the east, the Snake River Valley to the southwest, and Red Cone Peak and Webster Pass to the south.

Current Road Conditions
White River National Forest
Dillon Ranger District
680 River Parkway
Silverthorne, CO 80498
(970) 468-5400

A view of Santa Fe Peak Trail crossing a ridgeline

Map References

USFS   White River NF
USGS   Summit County #2
        Clear Creek County
Trails Illustrated, #104
The Roads of Colorado, p. 71
Colorado Atlas & Gazetteer, p. 38

Route Directions

▼ 0.0   From the Montezuma Snake River Fire
          Station, zero trip meter and proceed
          north on County 5 (FR 5).
          GPS: N 39°34.85′ W 105°52.03′

▼ 0.1 TR Intersection with Santa Fe Peak Road
          (FR 264).

▼ 0.2 SO Enter National Forest.
          GPS: N 39°34.96′ W 105°51.92′

▼ 0.9 SO Track on left—closed.
▼ 1.3 SO Mine ruins on right (private property).
▼ 1.4 SO Track to cabin (private property) on
          right; then mine ruins on right.
▼ 1.7 SO Track to mine on right (private property).
▼ 1.9 SO Mine on right.

▼ 2.6 SO Track on right. Stay on FR 264.
▼ 2.7 SO Timberline.
▼ 3.0 SO Quail Mine on right.
          GPS: N 39°34.83′ W 105°50.72′

▼ 3.3 SO View down onto Montezuma and

NC Trail #4: Santa Fe Peak Trail

Snake River Valley.

▼ 3.8   SO   Intersection. Track on right goes to Buena Vista Mine. Remain on FR 264.
GPS: N 39°34.67' W 105°50.33'

▼ 4.1   SO   Enter large plateau with spectacular 360-degree views.

▼ 4.6   SO   Turn-around and parking opportunity prior to shelf road.

▼ 4.8   SO   Ridge. Full-sized vehicles should stop at this point. Last good spot for turning around.
GPS: N 39°34.09' W 105°50.08'

▼ 5.1   BR   Last switchback.

▼ 5.2   Silver Wave Mine.
GPS: N 39°34.02' W 105°50.11'

NORTH-CENTRAL REGION TRAIL #5

Deer Creek Trail

STARTING POINT Montezuma

FINISHING POINT Three-way intersection of Deer Creek Road with Middle Fork of the Swan road and North Fork of the Swan/Saints John road

TOTAL MILEAGE 4.9 miles

UNPAVED MILEAGE 4.9 miles

DRIVING TIME 1/2 hour

ROUTE ELEVATION 10,300 feet to 12,400 feet

USUALLY OPEN Mid-June to late September

DIFFICULTY RATING 3

SCENIC RATING 7

Special Attractions

■ Provides access to an extensive network of 4WD trails.

■ A relatively easy road that provides a good introduction to roads in the area.

History

Montezuma, a silver camp named after the last Aztec emperor of Mexico, was founded in the 1860s. Henry Teller, who went on to serve as a U.S. senator for twenty-nine years, was possibly one of the first to locate silver in the area. The camp grew slowly, mainly because silver rather than gold was found and because of its inaccessibility. Ore shipments had to be made via the newly opened but difficult route across Argentine Pass, which led to high transportation costs.

When the Loveland and Webster Passes were built the late 1870s and silver mining was booming, Montezuma began to flourish. A regular stage traveled across both passes. Soon Montezuma was the focal point for the many mining camps in the district, offering supplies, a school, and entertainment such as dance halls, saloons, and poker games—which are said to have gone on twenty-four hours a day. Montezuma reached its peak population of about eight hundred residents around 1880, and the following year, the city was incorporated. In 1882, Montezuma's new trustees set about cleaning up the town, establishing fines for drunkenness, and outlawing gambling and prostitution.

Montezuma suffered greatly from the silver crash of 1893, although it never did become a ghost town. In 1958, a fire started at the Summit House hotel and blazed through town, completely destroying the hotel, the town hall, houses, garages, and other buildings. Almost half of the seventy-five residents were rendered homeless—a week before Christmas. In 1972, it lost its

The sign post at the end of Deer Creek Trail

Montezuma circa 1870

post office. Today, the town is a mixture of old and new buildings. The one-room schoolhouse, which operated from 1884 to 1958, still stands on a slope east of Main Street.

Franklin was the site of the headquarters of the Montezuma Silver Mining Company. It was deliberately located an appropriate distance from the jarring activity of the company's mines and was intended to become an elite community of the company's management. The first building was a large two-story house built for the mine superintendent. It was the showpiece of the town and was used to entertain visiting dignitaries. Today the foundations of the house are all that remain. At some point, a sawmill was also built at the site. Little else was ever built and the community was short-lived.

Description
Deer Creek Trail serves as the backbone for an extensive network of 4WD roads branching in all directions. Many of the roads are poorly marked, and navigation can be difficult. We strongly recommend that you use a copy of the *Trails Illustrated* map for the area. It is not entirely accurate but is much more up to date than any of the alternative maps.

Other than navigation, this route presents no major difficulties. The road is bumpy and includes some easy switchbacks, but the surface is sound.

Franklin is located just north of the intersection with North-Central #3: Webster Pass Trail. It is private property.

Current Road Conditions
White River National Forest
Dillon Ranger District
680 River Parkway
Silverthorne, CO 80498
(970) 468-5400

Map References
USFS White River NF
USGS Summit County #2 (incomplete)
Trails Illustrated, #104
The Roads of Colorado, p. 71
Colorado Atlas & Gazetteer, p. 38

Route Directions

▼ 0.0	From the Montezuma Snake River Fire Station, zero trip meter and proceed south on County 5 (FR 5).
1.0 ▲	End at the Montezuma Snake River Fire Station.
	GPS: N 39°34.85′ W 105°52.03′

NC Trail #5: Deer Creek Trail

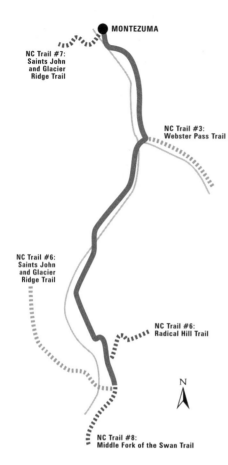

MONTEZUMA

NC Trail #7:
Saints John
and Glacier
Ridge Trail

NC Trail #3:
Webster Pass Trail

NC Trail #6:
Saints John
and Glacier
Ridge Trail

NC Trail #6:
Radical Hill Trail

N

NC Trail #8:
Middle Fork of the Swan Trail

▼ 0.7　SO Ruins of mine and log buildings.
0.3 ▲　SO Ruins of mine and log buildings.

▼ 1.0　SO Track on left is North-Central #3:
　　　　Webster Pass Trail. Town site of
　　　　Franklin. Zero trip meter.
0.0 ▲　Continue along County 5/FR 5.
　　　　GPS: N 39°34.08′ W 105°51.57′

▼ 0.0　Continue on County 5/FR 5.
3.9 ▲　SO Track on right is North-Central #3:
　　　　Webster Pass Trail. Town site of
　　　　Franklin. Zero trip meter.

▼ 0.4　SO Parking area. Cross over creek.
3.6 ▲　SO Cross over creek. Parking area.

▼ 0.9　SO Track on right dead-ends at mines.

3.1 ▲　SO Track on left dead-ends at mines.

▼ 1.0　SO Arapaho National Forest information
　　　　board. Seasonal closure gate.
2.9 ▲　SO Seasonal closure gate. Arapaho
　　　　National Forest information board.

▼ 1.5　SO Track to the right goes to mines.
2.4 ▲　SO Track to the left goes to mines.

▼ 1.6　SO Cross over Deer Creek. Track on the
　　　　left.
2.3 ▲　SO Track on right. Cross over Deer Creek.

▼ 1.7　SO Track on left goes to numerous
　　　　mines.
2.2 ▲　SO Track on right goes to numerous
　　　　mines.

▼ 2.0　SO Short track to the right.
1.9 ▲　SO Short track to the left.

▼ 2.2　BL Track on the right.
1.7 ▲　BR Track on the left.

▼ 3.4　BR Track on left is first turnoff to North-
　　　　Central #6: Radical Hill Trail (FR 286).
0.5 ▲　BL Track on right is second turnoff to
　　　　Radical Hill.

▼ 3.5　SO Track on left is second turnoff to
　　　　Radical Hill.
0.4 ▲　SO Track on right is first turnoff to
　　　　North-Central #6: Radical Hill Trail
　　　　(FR 286).

▼ 3.9　End at three-way intersection signpost
　　　　that points to the Middle Fork of the
　　　　Swan to the south, Montezuma to the
　　　　north, and the North Fork of the Swan
　　　　and Saints John to the west.
0.0 ▲　Begin at three-way intersection sign-
　　　　post that points to the Middle Fork of
　　　　the Swan to the south, Montezuma to
　　　　the north, and the North Fork of the
　　　　Swan and Saints John to the west.
　　　　Zero trip meter and take road toward
　　　　Montezuma.
　　　　GPS: N 39°31.24′ W 105°52.09′

Radical Hill Trail switchbacking down from Teller Mountain

Radical Hill Trail

STARTING POINT Intersection of North-Central #5: Deer Creek Trail and FR 286
FINISHING POINT Webster Pass Trail (FR 285)
TOTAL MILEAGE 2.5 miles
UNPAVED MILEAGE 2.5 miles
DRIVING TIME 3/4 hour
ROUTE ELEVATION 11,400 feet to 12,600 feet
USUALLY OPEN Mid-June to late September
DIFFICULTY RATING 6
SCENIC RATING 10

Special Attractions

- Very challenging 4WD trail.
- Interconnects with a network of other 4WD trails.
- Wonderful alpine scenery.

Description

This is a short, challenging road with a steep, loose, and very narrow shelf section. If you start at Deer Creek Trail, the difficult section is downhill. This route is the easier way of tackling it.

From Deer Creek Trail, the route commences a gentle ascent through a broad expanse of alpine tundra across the top of Radical Hill and over to Teller Mountain. After only about the first mile of the route, from the top of Teller Mountain, there is a particularly good view down into the Snake River Valley.

As you proceed from this point, the road turns, descends sharply, and switchbacks onto a very narrow shelf cut into the face of the mountain. The road is significantly eroded in spots as well as being off-camber and having a loose surface. As it curves around the mountain, it levels off and becomes wide enough to accommodate two vehicles when passing is necessary.

The balance of this short trail is a rough, rocky ride; but the worst is definitely over.

Current Road Conditions

White River National Forest
Dillon Ranger District
680 River Parkway
Silverthorne, CO 80498
(970) 468-5400

NC Trail #6: Radical Hill Trail

Map References

USFS White River NF
Trails Illustrated, #104
The Roads of Colorado, p. 71 (route incomplete)
Colorado Atlas & Gazetteer, p. 38 (route incomplete)

Route Directions

▼ 0.0   From intersection of Deer Creek Trail
        (FR 5) and Radical Hill Trail (FR 286),
        zero trip meter and turn onto FR 286.
2.5 ▲   End at intersection with North Central
        #5: Deer Creek Trail (FR 5).
        GPS: N 39°31.66' W 105°51.91'

▼ 0.1   SO   Track on right is alternative track to
             Deer Creek Trail.
2.4 ▲   BL   Track on left is alternative track to
             Deer Creek Trail.

▼ 0.9   SO   Scenic overlook and start of steep,
             narrow descent.
1.6 ▲   SO   Scenic overlook.

▼ 1.4   SO   Track on right to cabin.
1.1 ▲   SO   Track on left to cabin.
             GPS: N 39°32.05' W 105°51.18'

▼ 2.5   BL   Track on right, then end at intersection
             with North-Central #3: Webster Pass
             Trail.

0.0 ▲   At intersection of North-Central #3:
        Webster Pass Trail and Radical Hill Trail
        (FR 286), zero trip meter and proceed
        along FR 286.
        GPS: N 39°32.29' W 105°50.46'

Saints John and Glacier Mountain Trail

STARTING POINT Montezuma
FINISHING POINT Three-way intersection of
Deer Creek Trail with Middle Fork of
the Swan Trail and North Fork of the
Swan/Saints John road
TOTAL MILEAGE 7.2 miles
UNPAVED MILEAGE 7.1 miles
DRIVING TIME 1 1/2 hours
ROUTE ELEVATION 10,300 feet to 12,200 feet
USUALLY OPEN Mid-July to late September
DIFFICULTY RATING 4
SCENIC RATING 8

Special Attractions

■ Moderately challenging 4WD trail that
offers a mix of historic sites, varied trail
conditions, and excellent scenery.
■ Access to a network of 4WD trails.

History

Saints John was originally named Coleyville,
after John Coley, who located the first ore in
1863. Legend has it that hunters in the area
in 1861 ran out of bullets and resorted to
using pieces of rock in their guns. Two years
later, they were in Nevada and noticed a
great similarity between the rich ore they saw
there and the rocks that they had used as
ammunition. They contacted Coley, who set
up camp in the area and subsequently located
silver ore.

     A prospector named Bob Epsey is also
celebrated for an unusual strike. Suffering
from a hangover one day, Epsey lay down to
sleep it off under a shady tree. When he
awoke, he steadied himself by grasping a

The Wild Irishman Mine and site of the 1880s town

rock as he stood. When the rock broke off in Epsey's hand, he discovered in it a big chunk of solid ore.

The town was renamed Saints John by Freemasons who gave it the biblical name after John the Baptist and John the Evangelist. Saints John became a company town when it was taken over by the Boston Silver Mining Association, an East Coast company, in 1872. At great expense, the company erected a sophisticated milling and smelter work, complete with bricks imported from Europe. A few years later it was taken over by the Boston Mining Company. For such a remote mining town, Saints John had a 350-volume library (complete with regularly stocked newspapers from Boston and Europe), a boardinghouse, a dining hall, a company store, an assay office, various cabins, and a beautiful superintendent's house with elegant furnishings from Europe and the eastern United States. However, the mining companies did not allow a saloon, so the miners regularly traveled down the mountain to Montezuma, where they indulged to their hearts' content in brothels, saloons, and poker dens.

Poor access, harsh winters, and waning silver finds caused the decline of Saints John. Argentine and Webster Passes were impassable because of snow in the winter and at other times from rockslides. The post office was closed by 1881 and the town was deserted by the 1890s.

The Wild Irishman Mine was discovered by a New York City policeman named Michael Dulhaney, who came to Colorado and struck it rich in the late 1870s. It operated throughout the 1880s but remained just a camp and was never formally incorporated

Saints John in the 1870s

NC Trail #7: Saints John and Glacier Mountain Trail

TO GRIZZLY GULCH

County/FR 5

MONTEZUMA

County 275

Saints John Town Site

NC Trail #5: Deer Creek Trail

Wild Irishman Mine

General Teller Mine

NC Trail #5: Deer Creek Trail

NC Trail #6: Radical Hill Trail

N

NC Trail #9: North Fork of the Swan and Wise Mountain Trail

NC Trail #8: Middle Fork of the Swan Trail

tives and will prove helpful.

The road is rough in sections but sound. Some sections are steep but should prove well within the capability of a 4WD vehicle.

The road starts in Montezuma and ascends some switchbacks to the Saints John town site. It passes by the Wild Irishman Mine before switchbacking a steep slope onto the exposed Glacier Mountain. It then winds along the narrow ridge past the General Teller Mine and ends at the three-way intersection with Deer Creek Trail and the Middle Fork of the Swan Trail.

Current Road Conditions

White River National Forest
Dillon Ranger District
680 River Parkway
Silverthorne, CO 80498
(970) 468-5400

Map References

USFS White River NF
USGS Summit County #2 (incomplete)
Trails Illustrated, #104 (minor inaccuracies)
The Roads of Colorado, p. 71 (incomplete)
Colorado Atlas & Gazetteer, p. 38 (incomplete)

Route Directions

as a town. The camp had no church or school. Several cabins were situated around the mine so that the miners could be close to their work. The Wild Irishman camp is typical of a number of camps where men and their families worked during the mining boom. The ruins of the mine and the miner's cabins are still evident in a beautiful timberline meadow.

Description

This route offers a variety of attractions: the historic mining town of Saints John, old mines, creek crossings, and stunning alpine views.

As the roads in the area are frequently unmarked, we recommend that you take a copy of the *Trails Illustrated* map #104. It is not completely accurate but is much more up to date than any of the alterna-

▼ 0.0		From the Montezuma Snake River Fire Station, zero trip meter and proceed south on County 5 (FR 5).
7.2 ▲		End at the Montezuma Snake River Fire Station.
		GPS: N 39°34.85′ W 105°52.03′

▼ 150 yds	TR	Onto County 275 toward Saints John.
7.2 ▲	TL	Onto County 5 toward Montezuma.

▼ 0.2	SO	Track on left goes to the Equity Mine with old buildings in 0.2 miles.
7.0 ▲	SO	Track on right goes to the Equity Mine with old buildings.

▼ 0.5	SO	Enter Arapaho National Forest.
6.7 ▲	SO	Leave Arapaho National Forest.

▼ 0.6	SO	Track on right crosses Saints John

		Creek and leads to Grizzly Gulch.
6.6 ▲	SO	Track on left crosses Saints John Creek and leads to Grizzly Gulch.

▼ 1.3	SO	Town site of Saints John.
5.9 ▲	SO	Town site of Saints John.
		GPS: N 39°34.33′ W 105°52.85′

▼ 1.4	TR	Follow Jeep trail sign. Cross Saints John Creek. Track on left.
5.8 ▲	TL	Track on right. Cross Saints John Creek.

▼ 1.8	SO	Cross Saints John Creek. Arapaho National Forest information board. Seasonal closure gate.
5.4 ▲	SO	Seasonal closure gate. Cross Saints John Creek.
		GPS: N 39°34.00′ W 105°53.23′

▼ 2.3	TL	T-Intersection. Right goes to camping possibilities. Cross creek.
4.9 ▲	TR	Cross creek. Track on left goes to camping possibilities.

▼ 2.5	SO	Creek crossing.
4.7 ▲	SO	Creek crossing.

▼ 2.8	SO	Wild Irishman Mine is approximately 100 yards off the road on left.
4.4 ▲	SO	Wild Irishman Mine is approximately 100 yards off the road on right.

▼ 2.9	SO	Wild Irishman Mine tailings.
4.3 ▲	SO	Wild Irishman Mine tailings.

▼ 3.0	TR	Trail on left goes to Wild Irishman Mine.
4.2 ▲	TL	Trail on right goes to Wild Irishman Mine.

▼ 3.5	SO	Short trail on left.
3.7 ▲	SO	Short trail on right.

▼ 3.7	SO	Trail on left.
3.5 ▲	SO	Trail on right.

▼ 3.8	SO	General Teller Mine remains on left exposed on mountain ridge.
3.4 ▲	SO	General Teller Mine remains on right exposed on mountain ridge.

▼ 4.5	SO	Track on left dead-ends at old mine.
2.7 ▲	SO	Track on right dead-ends at old mine.

▼ 6.5	TL	T-intersection. Track on right is North-Central #9: North Fork of the Swan and Wise Mountain Trail.
0.7 ▲	TR	Intersection. Straight ahead leads to North-Central #9: North Fork of the Swan and Wise Mountain Trail
		GPS: N 39°31.39′ W 105°52.89′

▼ 7.2		End at T-intersection. Signpost shows Montezuma to the left (North-Central #5: Deer Creek Trail), and Middle Fork of the Swan to the right (North-Central #8).
0.0 ▲		Begin at three-way intersection signpost that points to the Middle Fork of the Swan to the south, Montezuma to the north, and North Fork of the Swan and Saints John to the west. Zero trip meter and take road toward Saints John.
		GPS: N 39°31.24′ W 105°52.09′

NORTH-CENTRAL REGION TRAIL #8

Middle Fork of the Swan Trail

STARTING POINT Three-way intersection of Deer Creek Trail with Middle Fork of the Swan Trail and North Fork of the Swan/Saints John road

FINISHING POINT Breckenridge at intersection of Colorado 9 and Tiger Road

TOTAL MILEAGE 12.7 miles

UNPAVED MILEAGE 11.8 miles

DRIVING TIME 1 hour

ROUTE ELEVATION 9,250 feet to 12,200 feet

USUALLY OPEN Mid-June to early October

DIFFICULTY RATING 5

SCENIC RATING 8

Special Attractions
- Interesting, though unsightly, remains of extensive placer mining by dredge boats.
- Beautiful, wooded valley along the upper

The benign-looking uphill section that can become impassable in wet conditions

reaches of the Middle Fork of the Swan River.
- Challenging uphill section.
- Access to a network of 4WD trails.

History

Towns along this route were Swandyke, Tiger, Swan City, Delaware Flats, and Braddocks.

Swandyke boomed briefly in the late 1890s, considerably later than most other Colorado mining camps. The gold camp was divided into two sections called Swandyke and Upper Swandyke, about a mile apart.

Tiger township in about 1940

Stagecoach service connected the camp to Breckenridge and over Webster Pass to Jefferson; and from there, railroad service ran regularly to Denver. Swandyke's population peaked at about five hundred in 1899, when the post office was set up. Few of the miners remained through the winter. During the camp's first winter, in 1898–1899, extremely heavy snowfalls led to a number of snowslides, which destroyed most of the buildings in the new town. One avalanche carried Swandyke's mill down one side of the mountain and across a deep gulch, leaving the wreckage on the opposite mountainside. Swandyke was a ghost town by 1902, although the post office was not officially closed until 1910.

Tiger, another mining camp, was established following discovery of the Tiger Lode in 1864. Soon, additional discoveries were made in the area. Shortly after the turn of the century, the Royal Tiger Mining Company was formed and bought up most of the mines. It established the company town of Tiger and provided well for the miners. They had free electricity, steam heat, and a school for the children; the company even held regular dances and free movie hows. The mine closed in 1940 and Tiger quickly became a ghost town. Because the town was much younger than most ghost towns, the buildings remained in good condition, and in the 1960s, the town was reoccupied as a hippy commune. However, authorities responded by burning it to the ground in 1973.

About a half-mile past the site of Tiger, Swan City sprang to life in May 1880 and within three months it had a post office, a general store, a saloon, and a hotel; but within ten years the gold mines were no longer profitable and the town was deserted. Although mining in the area was revitalized with the arrival of dredge boats, Swan City was obliterated—buried beneath tons of rubble left by the dredges.

A miner's cabin beside the Middle Fork of the Swan River

Delaware Flats was established in 1860 during the initial gold rush to the area. This was eight years prior to the Kit Carson Treaty, when the district was ceded by the Ute. Within a year, the town had a post office and several hundred prospectors. In 1875, the name of the town was changed to Preston. The post office closed in 1880, and twenty years later, the dredge boats completely buried the site. Today, the golf course is on the western end of the reclaimed town site.

Braddocks, at the intersection of Tiger Road and Colorado 9, was founded by Dave Braddocks who operated the local stage line and livery stable. In 1884, the Denver, South Park & Pacific Railroad built a station at the location.

Description

This route commences at the three-way intersection at the end of Deer Creek Trail and travels along an alpine ridge toward the headwaters of the Middle Fork of the Swan River.

At the 0.8-mile point, there is a sign to Hall Valley. This road does not go through to Hall Valley but goes to an overlook of the valley. It is a worthwhile side-trip that not only provides a wonderful view down into the valley but also offers a spectacular panoramic view across the top of Handcart

Gulch to Red Cone Peak and the trail descending from it (North-Central #2) to Webster Pass. The shelf road from Webster Pass that leads down into Handcart Gulch (North-Central #1) is also clearly visible from this vantage point.

Shortly after, the road travels along the side of the mountain. The road is significantly off-camber for some distance before starting the steep descent down to the valley floor. The surface during the descent is quite loose in sections and can be considerably looser if wet. Traveling uphill under such conditions in a stock vehicle can be nearly impossible. It is for this short section of road that the route warrants its difficulty rating; otherwise a rating of 3 would be more appropriate. The road continues along the extremely attractive Middle Fork of the Swan River before intersecting with North-Central #10: Georgia Pass Trail.

From this point, the road is easily accessible to 2WD vehicles as it threads a path through an almost continual line of huge tailing dumps from the dredge mining in the early 1900s. At the 3.6-mile point from the intersection with Georgia Pass Trail, in a pond among tailings, lie the remains of the mining boat Tiger Dredge #1.

The route ends at the intersection of Colorado 9 and Tiger Road (at the

NC Trail #8: Middle Fork of the Swan Trail

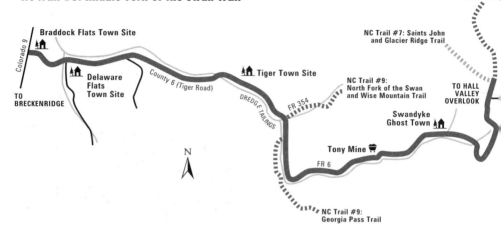

Highlands at Breckenridge public golf course). This intersection was the site of the towns of Delaware Flats and Braddocks, named for the Denver, South Park & Pacific Railroad station that was located there.

Current Road Conditions

White River National Forest
Dillon Ranger District
680 River Parkway
Silverthorne, CO 80498
(970) 468-5400

Map References

USFS   White River NF
USGS   Summit County #2 (incomplete)
Trails Illustrated, #104 (minor inaccuracies), #109
The Roads of Colorado, p. 71 (incomplete)
Colorado Atlas & Gazetteer, p. 38 (incomplete)

Route Directions

▼ 0.0   Begin at three-way intersection signpost that points to Middle Fork of the Swan to the south, Montezuma to the north, and North Fork of the Swan and Saints John to the west. Zero trip meter and take the road toward Middle Fork of the Swan.

6.6 ▲   End at three-way intersection signpost that points to Middle Fork of the Swan

to the south, Montezuma to the north, and North Fork of the Swan and Saints John to the west.
GPS: N 39°31.24' W 105°52.09'

0.5   SO Track on left.
6.1 ▲   SO Track on right.

▼ 0.6   TR Track on left, followed by an intersection. Sign to Hall Valley (this side road ends at a scenic overlook in 0.8 miles). Proceed toward Middle Fork of the Swan on FR 220.

6.0 ▲   TL T-intersection. Hall Valley scenic overlook is to the right. Follow sign to Montezuma. Then pass a small track on right.
GPS: N 39°30.83' W 105°51.74'

▼ 1.5   SO Track on left.
5.1 ▲   SO Track on right.

▼ 1.8   SO Log cabin ruins on right.
4.9 ▲   SO Log cabin ruins on left.

▼ 2.2   SO Cross through creek.
4.4 ▲   SO Cross through creek.

▼ 2.4   SO Track on right.
4.2 ▲   SO Track on left.

t 2.7   SO Deserted log cabin on right. Site of Swandyke.

DREDGE BOAT PLACER-MINING

Gold and silver deposits are frequently found together. They are formed when molten minerals are forced up from deep within the earth into the bedrock. Usually gold and silver also exist with other minerals such as pyrite (fool's gold) and galena (which has a silvery appearance). Commonly, the host rock is quartz.

Over time, erosion breaks down the rock deposits and the gold is freed and left in pure form. Water then disperses the free gold along streambeds. In its free form, gold exists in a variety of shapes: nuggets, scale, shot, grains, dust. These free deposits are known as "placers" when the gold is found in streambeds or along stream banks. A deposit of gold that is still contained in a rock formation is called a "lode."

Because placers are relatively easy to find, they are normally the first gold deposits discovered in any area. Miners typically follow the placers upstream to the mother lode.

Placer mining is the simplest form of mining operations, since it merely involves separating the free gold from the dirt, mud, or gravel with which it is mixed. At its simplest, the process involves either simple panning or sluicing to process a larger volume (which is based on the same principle as panning). Placer mining was known as "poor man's mining" because panning a creek could be done with very little capital. Colorado's placer production has been nearly all gold.

Dredging, an expansion of these methods, processed huge volumes of rock and required considerable capital. Dredge mining utilizes a power-driven chain of small buckets mounted on a barge, leaving in its wake squalid piles of washed rock to mark its course for decades to come. Processing tons of rock and soil quickly, dredges overcame the problem of large quantities of low-grade gravel. Dredges could move up to three-quarters of a million yards of earth per annum.

Four huge dredge boats were used to placer-mine the Swan River for gold up until 1904. In 1899, workers assembled these boats on-site from two hundred tons of components that were freighted in from Milwaukee and huge beams of West Coast redwood brought from Oregon.

The mountainous, unsightly gravel mounds along Swan River are tailings dumped by these boats. The remains of the last dredge boat are also along the route, and better preserved remains of another boat are located in French's Gulch.

Gold dredge #3 near Breckenridge

3.9 ▲   SO Deserted log cabin on left. Site of
             Swandyke.
             GPS: N 39°30.49′ W 105°53.50′

▼ 3.0   SO Cross through creek, then track on
             right.
3.6 ▲   SO Track on left, then cross through creek.

▼ 3.4   SO Track on left.
3.2 ▲   SO Track on right.

▼ 3.8   SO Cabin ruins on right.
2.8 ▲   SO Cabin ruins on left.

▼ 4.0   SO Private track to the Tony Mine on
             right.
2.6 ▲   SO Private track to the Tony Mine on
             left.
             GPS: N 39°30.14′ W 105°54.71′

▼ 4.1   SO Track on left.
2.5 ▲   SO Track on right.

▼ 4.8   SO Track on left.
1.8 ▲   SO Track on right.

▼ 5.9   SO Seasonal gate.
0.7 ▲   SO Seasonal gate.

▼ 6.6   SO Road on left goes to North-Central
             #10: Georgia Pass Trail. Zero trip
             meter.
0.0 ▲   Continue straight on.
             GPS: N 39°30.39′ W 105°56.71′

▼ 0.0   Continue straight ahead on County 6
             (Tiger Road) toward Breckenridge.
6.1 ▲   SO Road on right is North-Central #10:
             Georgia Pass Trail. Signpost points to
             Middle Fork straight ahead and South
             Fork (Georgia Pass) to the right. Zero
             trip meter.

▼ 0.5   BL Cross bridge. Road on right is North-
             Central #9: North Fork of the Swan
             and Wise Mountain Trail.
5.6 ▲   BR Road on left is North-Central #9: North
             Fork of the Swan and Wise Mountain
             Trail. Cross bridge.

▼ 1.5   SO Road on left. Tiger town site on
             right.
4.6 ▲   SO Road on right. Tiger town site on
             left.
             GPS: N 39°31.37′ W 105°57.69′

▼ 3.6   SO Parking area for viewing of historic
             dredge boat on right.
2.5 ▲   SO Parking area for viewing historic
             dredge boat on left.

▼ 6.1   End at intersection with Colorado 9.
             Breckenridge is to the left.
0.0 ▲   At intersection of Route 9 and County
             6 (Tiger Road), 3.2 miles north of
             Breckenridge Visitor Center, zero trip
             meter and proceed east along Tiger
             Road. This intersection is marked with
             a sign for the Breckenridge Public Golf
             Course.
             GPS: N 39°31.95′ W 106°02.58′

North Fork of the Swan and Wise Mountain Trail

STARTING POINT Intersection of North-Central
#8: Middle Fork of the Swan Trail and
FR 354

FINISHING POINT Intersection of North-Central
#7: Saints John and Glacier Mountain
Trail and FR 356

TOTAL MILEAGE 9.6 Miles

UNPAVED MILEAGE 9.6 Miles

DRIVING TIME 1 1/2 hours

ROUTE ELEVATION 10,000 feet to 12,400 feet

USUALLY OPEN Early July to early October

DIFFICULTY RATING 6 (5 traveling the reverse
direction)

SCENIC RATING 9

Special Attractions

■ Spectacular, expansive views.

■ Town site of Rexford and views of mine
and cabin ruins.

■ Challenging, short, steep section along the
trail.

■ Access to a network of 4WD roads.

History

In 1880 Daniel Patrick discovered the
Rochester lode. Two mines, the Rochester
King and the Rochester Queen, were developed the following year by the Rexford
Mining Corporation. To enable development of the mines in this remote location,
the company also built the town of Rexford
on land it owned. A mill was built near the
mines to process the ore before shipment to
a smelter in Denver. Within two years,
declining production and high costs closed
the mine and the town was deserted.

Rexford had a post office from 1882 until
the following year as well as a general store, a
saloon, a boardinghouse for the miners, and
several cabins. At its peak, the town had a
twice-weekly mail service from Montezuma.
Several buildings are still evident at Rexford
but all have, at least partially, collapsed.

The remains of Rexford in 1961

About three-quarters of a mile before Rexford, two buildings that were used by loggers when they were working the area are still standing. They were built after the demise of Rexford.

Description

The road commences at the intersection with North-Central #8: Middle Fork of the Swan Trail. Initially, the road is graded but becomes rough after a mile of so. Nonetheless, it remains easy for the first 2.2 miles; good backcountry camping sites exist along this section. However, after the turnoff for Rexford, water crossings, short sections that can be muddy, and progressively steeper sections make a 4WD necessary.

After returning from the side road to Rexford, the main trail climbs above timberline and goes past a mine before intersecting a trail to a small cabin perched atop Wise Mountain, which, although very exposed to the elements, is still used. Turning to the left, the trail crosses the treeless ridgeline for about half a mile before encountering the most difficult section of the route: a very steep, loose section that transitions between two ridgelines. Until this point, the trail would have only been rated a 5 for difficulty, but this section increases the rating to a 6. (Going downhill, the rating remains a 5.)

From Wise Mountain, there are sweeping views in all directions. In particular, spectacular views are afforded down into the Middle Fork of the Swan River Valley and north toward Saints John.

The road ends at the intersection with North-Central #7: Saints John and Glacier Mountain Trail. From this point, you can select from a number of routes leading to Montezuma or Breckenridge.

Current Road Conditions

White River National Forest
Dillon Ranger District
680 River Parkway
Silverthorne, CO 80498
(970) 468-5400

Map References

USFS White River NF
USGS Summit County #2 (incomplete)
Trails Illustrated, #104
The Roads of Colorado, p. 71 (incomplete)
Colorado Atlas & Gazetteer, p. 38 (incomplete)

NC Trail #9: North Fork of the Swan and Wise Mountain Trail

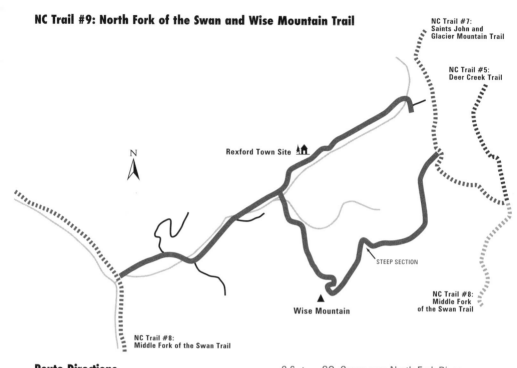

NC Trail #7:
Saints John and
Glacier Mountain Trail

NC Trail #5:
Deer Creek Trail

N

Rexford Town Site

STEEP SECTION

NC Trail #8:
Middle Fork
of the Swan Trail

Wise Mountain

NC Trail #8:
Middle Fork of the Swan Trail

Route Directions

▼ 0.0   From North-Central #8: Middle Fork of the Swan Trail (County 6/Tiger Road), zero trip meter and proceed along FR 354, following sign to North Fork.

2.2 ▲   End at intersection with Tiger Road, which is also North-Central #8: Middle Fork of the Swan Trail. Right goes toward Breckenridge and left continues the Middle Fork Trail and also goes toward Georgia Pass.
       GPS: N 39°30.80' W 105°56.79'

▼ 0.5   SO   Track on left.
1.7 ▲   SO   Track on right.

▼ 0.6   SO   Seasonal gate.
1.6 ▲   SO   Seasonal gate.

▼ 0.9   SO   Gated track on right.
1.2 ▲   SO   Gated track on left.

▼ 1.5   SO   Gated track on right.
0.7 ▲   SO   Gated track on left.

▼ 1.6   SO   Cross over North Fork River.

0.6 ▲   SO   Cross over North Fork River.

▼ 1.7   BR   Fork in road. Left is gated in 0.1 miles.
0.4 ▲   SO   Fork in road. Right is gated in 0.1 miles.
       GPS: N 39°31.43' W 105°55.23'

▼ 2.2   BL   Fork in road. Remains of two cabins from a logging camp. Zero trip meter.
0.0 ▲   Continue along track toward the Middle Fork of the Swan River.
       GPS: N 39°31.65' W 105°54.75'

▼ 0.0   Proceed along side road toward Rexford. (This road dead-ends, so you will have to return to this spot.)
4.4 ▲   SO   After returning to the intersection beside the two logging cabins, proceed straight on. Track on the left toward Wise Mountain. Zero trip meter.

▼ 0.4   SO   Cabin on left.
4.0 ▲   SO   Cabin on right.
       GPS: N 39°31.90' W 105°54.54'

▼ 0.7   SO   Site of Rexford. Numerous cabin ruins

on left and right.

▲ 3.7 | SO | Rexford town site.
GPS: N 39°32.04' W 105°54.25'

▼ 1.8 | SO | Cabin ruins on right.
▲ 2.6 | SO | Cabin ruins on left.
GPS: N 39°32.48' W 105°53.35'

▼ 1.9 | BR | Track on left. Cross through creek.
▲ 2.5 | BL | Cross through creek. Track on right.

▼ 2.0 | BL | Fork in the road.
▲ 2.4 | BR | Fork in the road.
GPS: N 39°32.49' W 105°53.18'

▼ 2.2 | UT | End of track at mine.
▲ 2.2 | UT | End of track at mine.
GPS: N 39°32.40' W 105°53.18'

▼ 2.4 | BR | Fork in the road.
▲ 2.0 | BL | Fork in the road.

▼ 2.5 | BL | Cross through creek. Track on right.
▲ 1.9 | BR | Track on left. Cross through creek.

▼ 2.6 | SO | Cabin ruins on left.
▲ 1.8 | SO | Cabin ruins on right.
GPS: N 39°32.48' W 105°53.35'

▼ 3.7 | SO | Rexford town site.
▲ 0.7 | SO | Site of Rexford. Numerous cabin ruins on left and right.

▼ 4.0 | SO | Cabin on right.
▲ 0.4 | SO | Cabin on left.

▼ 4.4 | TL | Upon returning to the intersection beside the two old logging cabins, zero trip meter and turn left.
▲ 0.0 | | Turn right and proceed along the side road to Rexford. (This road dead-ends, so you will have to return to this spot.)
GPS: N 39°31.65' W 105°54.75'

▼ 0.0 | | Cross through the North Fork of the Swan and proceed toward Wise Mountain.
▲ 1.3 | TR | Cross through the North Fork of the Swan. Intersection and the remains of two logging cabins. Zero trip meter.

▼ 0.1 | SO | Cross through creek.
▲ 1.2 | SO | Cross through creek.

▼ 0.3 | SO | Cabin on right.
▲ 1.1 | SO | Cabin on left.

▼ 1.3 | SO | Mine on left.
▲ 0.1 | SO | Mine on right.
GPS: N 39°30.87' W 105°54.17'

▼ 1.4 | TL | Intersection. Mine on Wise Mountain and cabin are 0.1 miles to the right. Deer Creek is to the left. Zero trip meter.
▲ 0.0 | | Proceed toward North Fork.
GPS: N 39°30.80' W 105°54.13'

▼ 0.0 | | Proceed toward Deer Creek.
▲ 1.6 | TR | Intersection. Mine on Wise Mountain and cabin are 0.1 miles straight ahead. North Fork is to the right. Zero trip meter.

▼ 1.6 | SO | End at intersection with North-Central #7: Saints John and Glacier Mountain Trail on left.
▲ 0.0 | | From North-Central #7: Saints John and Glacier Mountain Trail, zero trip meter and proceed south on FR 356 toward North Fork and Wise Mountain.
GPS: N 39°31.39' W 105°52.89'

NORTH-CENTRAL REGION TRAIL #10

Georgia Pass Trail

STARTING POINT North-Central #8: Middle Fork of the Swan Trail and FR 355

FINISHING POINT Intersection of US 285 and County 35 in Jefferson

TOTAL MILEAGE 16.1 miles

UNPAVED MILEAGE 16.1 miles

DRIVING TIME 1 1/2 hours

ROUTE ELEVATION 9,500 feet to 11,585 feet

USUALLY OPEN Mid-June to late September

DIFFICULTY RATING 4

SCENIC RATING 7

Special Attractions

- Historic route and mining sites.
- Parkville Cemetery.
- Can be combined with North-Central #3: Webster Pass Trail to form a loop.

History

Before the establishment of the Colorado Territory in 1861, Georgia Pass traversed the boundary of the Utah and Kansas Territories. Crossing over the Continental Divide, the pass was traveled heavily by both the Ute and after their migration south from Montana and Wyoming in the early 1800s, the Arapaho. The Arapaho were the more hostile of the two tribes. Many early prospectors and setters to avoided the pass when they were in the vicinity. John Frémont visited the area in 1844, but he chose to detour to Hoosier Pass to steer clear of the Arapaho.

Despite the threat of attack by the Arapaho, many early prospectors braved the route. It was heavily used in the 1859 gold rush to the Blue River diggings, which

The Georgia Pass Trail approaching the summit

included the mining camps of Breckenridge, Lincoln City, and Frisco on the Blue River; Tiger and Parkville on the Swan River; and Montezuma, Saints John, and Argentine in the Snake River area.

Breckenridge produced Colorado's largest gold nugget, the fourteen-pound "Tom's Baby," which disappeared a few years after it was discovered and was presumed stolen to be broken down or melted. But in 1971, officials of the Denver Museum of Natural History found it in a box that was thought to contain dinosaur bones. The nugget is now on exhibit at the museum.

The first recorded wagon crossing over Georgia Pass was in November 1861; later that year, approval for a toll road was granted. A stagecoach service operated across the pass between Swandyke and Jefferson.

Description

The route commences at the intersection with North-Central #8: Middle Fork of the Swan Trail. Initially, the road is easily accessible to 2WD vehicles but gradually becomes more difficult.

Soon after the start, the route passes the town site of Parkville, the main mining camp in Summit County during the gold rush of the 1860s. All that remains of the once bustling town of ten thousand is the cemetery, which can be reached via a short walking track.

After Parkville, the road forks. This route follows the left fork; the right fork turns toward Georgia Gulch and leads to Breckenridge via Georgia Gulch, American Gulch, French's Gulch, and the town site of Lincoln City.

From here to the summit, stay on the main road rather than follow any of the intersecting roads—most are dead ends. The summit is an open, grassy saddle with good views of Mount Guyot to the west.

The south side of the pass down to Jefferson is narrow initially but much easier than the north side. From Jefferson, it is 16 miles southwest to Fairplay, 23 miles east to Bailey, and 8.4 miles northeast to the turnoff for North-Central #1: Handcart Gulch Trail.

The summit of Georgia Pass

Current Road Conditions

White River National Forest
Dillon Ranger District
680 River Parkway
Silverthorne, CO 80498
(970) 468-5400

Map References

USFS White River NF
Pike NF
USGS Summit County #2 (incomplete)
Park County #1
Trails Illustrated, #104, #105, #108, #109
The Roads of Colorado, pp. 70–71
Colorado Atlas & Gazetteer, pp. 38, 48

Route Directions

▼ 0.0   Begin at intersection of County 6/Tiger Road (North-Central #8: Middle Fork of the Swan Trail) and FR 355. Zero trip meter and proceed toward Georgia Pass on FR 355.

4.4 ▲   End at intersection of County 6 (Tiger Road). This is North-Central #8: Middle Fork of the Swan Trail.

GPS: N 39°30.37' W 105°56.73'

▼ 0.6   SO   Cross through creek bed. Town site of Parkville on right.

3.8 ▲   SO   Cross through creek bed. Town site of Parkville on left.

▼ 0.7   SO   Walking track on left. Parkville Cemetery and Masonic marker are about 150 yards down the trail.

3.7 ▲   SO   Walking track on right. Parkville Cemetery and Masonic marker are about 150 yards down the trail.

▼ 0.8   BL   Fork in the road. Track on right goes to Georgia Gulch. Cross bridge.

3.5 ▲   BR   Cross bridge to intersection. Track on the left goes to Georgia Gulch.

GPS: N 39°27.70' W 105°56.82'

▼ 1.5   SO   Log cabin on left.

2.8 ▲   SO   Log cabin on right.

▼ 2.2   SO   White cabin (private property) on right.

2.2 ▲   SO   White cabin (private property) on left.

▼ 2.7   BL   Follow FR 355. Track on right crosses through creek.

1.7 ▲   BR   Track on left crosses through creek.

GPS: N 39°28.73' W 105°55.33'

▼ 2.8 BL Cross through creek.
1.6 ▲ BR Cross through creek.

▼ 2.9 BR Fork in road. Take right fork and cross through creek.
1.5 ▲ BL Cross through creek. Track on right.

▼ 3.0 BR Fork in road. Track on left.
1.4 ▲ SO Track on right.

▼ 3.1 BR Track on left.
1.2 ▲ BL Track on right.

▼ 3.3 SO Seasonal closure gate.
1.1 ▲ SO Seasonal closure gate.
GPS: N 39°28.31′ W 105°55.08′

▼ 3.5 TL Intersection.
0.9 ▲ TR Intersection.
GPS: N 39°28.15′ W 105°55.18′

▼ 3.6 SO Cross over creek.
0.8 ▲ SO Cross over creek.

▼ 4.3 SO Intersection. Proceed up hill.
0.1 ▲ SO Intersection.

▼ 4.4 SO Summit of Georgia Pass. North-Central #11: Glacier Peak Trail is to the left. Zero trip meter at the summit marker.
0.0 ▲ Continue along Georgia Pass Road.
GPS: N 39°27.50′ W 105°54.98′

▼ 0.0 Continue toward Jefferson and Michigan Creek Campground on FR 54.
11.7 ▲ SO Summit of Georgia Pass. North-Central #11: Glacier Peak Trail is to the left. Zero trip meter at the summit marker.

▼ 0.2 SO Track on right.
11.5 ▲ BR Track on left.

▼ 0.3 SO Track on right.
11.4 ▲ SO Track on left.

▼ 0.5 SO Cabin on right.
11.2 ▲ SO Cabin on left.

▼ 2.3 SO Cross over creek.

GOLD RUSH LED TO A STRUGGLE FOR THE LAND

In 1859, the Pikes Peak gold rush erupted, and thousands of white prospectors and settlers poured across the eastern plains of Colorado. This land was controlled by two Indian tribes—the Cheyenne and the Arapaho. From his appointment in 1862, Territorial Governor John Evans sought to open up eastern Colorado to the white settlers; but neither tribe would agree to sell their lands and move to reservations. Evans decided to force the issue through what became known as the Cheyenne-Arapaho War, or the Colorado War, of 1864–1865.

Territorial military commander Colonel John Chivington launched an attack against the Indians, destroying their villages. In response, the Indians raided white settlements. This produced public support for a policy of extermination and led to the Sand Creek Massacre, which left two hundred Indians dead. After many more encounters, a treaty was negotiated in 1865; but the last battle on the Colorado plains was not fought until 1869.

During this period, the Ute, who controlled nearly all Colorado land west of the Front Range, maintained an uneasy peace with the whites who were slowly encroaching on their lands. The initial fur trapping and prospecting had not greatly affected the Ute way of life, but numerous gold discoveries from 1858 to 1860 led to more incursions of white settlers into Ute territory.

In 1868, in response to the influx of miners and continued pressure for land to settle, a treaty known as the Kit Carson Treaty was negotiated by Chief Ouray, whereby the Ute gave up their land in the central Rockies and San Luis Valley and agreed to be settled on the remaining 16 million acres of their land in western Colorado.

▼9.4 ▲	SO	Cross over creek.
▼ 3.6	SO	Numerous camping spots on left. Cross over creek.
8.1 ▲	SO	Cross over creek.
▼ 5.3	SO	FR 136 on right.
6.4 ▲	SO	FR 136 on left.
▼ 5.9	SO	USFS Michigan Creek Campground on right.
5.8 ▲	SO	USFS Michigan Creek Campground on left. **GPS: N 39°24.68′ W 105°53.01′**
▼ 6.5	TR	Intersection.
5.2 ▲	TL	Intersection.
▼ 6.9	SO	Leave Pike National Forest.
4.8 ▲	SO	Enter Pike National Forest.
▼ 8.9	BL	Intersection.
2.8 ▲	BR	Intersection.
▼ 9.8	SO	Intersection. Jefferson Lake to the left.
1.9 ▲	SO	Intersection. Jefferson Lake to the right.
▼ 11.7		End at intersection of US 285 and County 35 in Jefferson.

0.0 ▲   At intersection of US 285 and County 35 in Jefferson, zero trip meter and proceed along County 35 toward Georgia Pass. This intersection is marked with a National Forest sign to Jefferson Lake Road and Michigan Creek Road.
GPS: N 39°22.67′ W 105°48.01′

NORTH-CENTRAL REGION TRAIL #11

Glacier Peak Trail

STARTING POINT Summit of North-Central #10: Georgia Pass Trail
FINISHING POINT S.O.B. Hill
TOTAL MILEAGE 4.2 miles (one-way)
UNPAVED MILEAGE 4.2 miles
DRIVING TIME 1 hour
ROUTE ELEVATION 11,000 feet to 11,585 feet
USUALLY OPEN Mid-July to mid-September
DIFFICULTY RATING 5
SCENIC RATING 8

Special Attractions

■ Short side road from Georgia Pass.
■ Great scenery, particularly the view of Mount Guyot.

A pickup truck (circled) that has crashed down the mountain

Description

This trail is an interesting side road from Georgia Pass. At the summit of the pass there are a number of trails and it can be difficult to distinguish one from another. The Glacier Peak Trail departs to the northeast, heading directly away from the face of the information board at the summit.

Initially, it is rough but not difficult. A little more than half a mile from the summit two 4WD roads intersect to the right. The road to the right is easy and offers a mile or so of scenic alpine meadow to explore. The center, shorter road climbs the hill and provides a very good view of the area. It is more difficult than the other side road.

The main route continues to the left. As you continue along this rough, off-camber, narrow shelf road, there is a great view across to Mount Guyot. The ski runs of Breckenridge and Dillon Reservoir can also be sighted in the distance. Although rough, the surface of the road is mostly embedded rock and is generally sound.

As you continue, the road descends back below timberline. At one point, as you travel along a narrow shelf road, you can look across the valley and glimpse (between the trees on the left-hand side of the road), a turquoise pickup that has crashed down the slope and landed near the bottom of the valley.

Toward the end of the route, after you pass some alpine meadows, there is a creek crossing with a short steep descent and an even steeper ascent. This is the most difficult section. At this point we end the directions because the road deteriorates dramatically as it descends the aptly named S.O.B. Hill, which has a difficulty rating of 8. This is an extremely challenging, steep slope interspersed with many large boulders. To proceed further would certainly risk damage to any larger, stock vehicle.

If you proceed despite the risk, you will come out close to an intersection with North-Central #8: Middle Fork of the Swan Trail. Once down S.O.B. Hill, the road crosses through the Middle Fork of the Swan River and then, almost immediately, intersects the trail between the Tony Mine and Swandyke town site.

Current Road Conditions

White River National Forest
Dillon Ranger District
680 River Parkway
Silverthorne, CO 80498
(970) 468-5400

Map References

USFS White River NF
USGS Summit County #2 (incomplete)
Trails Illustrated, #104, #109
The Roads of Colorado, p. 71 (incomplete)
Colorado Atlas & Gazetteer, p. 38 (incomplete)

C Trail #11: Glacier Peak Trail

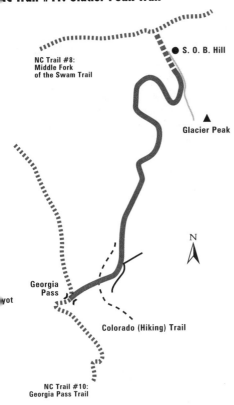

NC Trail #8:
Middle Fork
of the Swam Trail

S. O. B. Hill

Glacier Peak

Georgia
Pass

yot

Colorado (Hiking) Trail

NC Trail #10:
Georgia Pass Trail

N

Route Directions

▼ 0.0   From the summit marker on North-Central #10: Georgia Pass Trail, zero trip meter and proceed toward sign for Glacier Ridge and Colorado Trail on FR 268.
N39°27.50′ W105°54.98′

▼ 0.4   SO   Colorado Trail hiking trail crosses track.
▼ 0.7   BL   Intersection with FR 2681 and 2682.
▼ 2.4   SO   Short track on right to a scenic view down into Missouri Gulch. Zero trip meter.
N39°29.14′ W105°53.81′

▼ 0.0   Continue along track.
▼ 1.1   SO   On mountainside to the left, you can see a turquoise-color car that has crashed down the slope.
▼ 1.2   SO   Cross through creek.

▼ 1.4   SO   Several cabin ruins on left.
▼ 1.6   SO   Cross through creek and cabin ruins on left. Then cross through another creek.
▼ 1.7   SO   Cross through creek and climb steep embankment.
▼ 1.8   SO   End here unless you want to venture down S.O.B. Hill. The road continues to the right but is not passable at the level of this book.
N39°29.75′ W105°53.68′ (Estimated)

NORTH-CENTRAL REGION TRAIL #12

Boreas Pass Trail

STARTING POINT Breckenridge Visitor Information Center
FINISHING POINT Como at the intersection of US 285 and County/FR 33
TOTAL MILEAGE 21.3 miles
UNPAVED MILEAGE 17.0 miles
DRIVING TIME 1 1/4 hours
ROUTE ELEVATION 9,600 feet to 11,481 feet
USUALLY OPEN Late May to mid-October
DIFFICULTY RATING 1
SCENIC RATING 8

Special Attractions

■ Travel the route of a famous old narrow-gauge railway, which in its time was the highest in the United States.
■ Narrow railway cuttings, fine views, and the sites of many old mining camps.
■ In fall, excellent views of the changing aspens.

History

This pass was called by many names—Ute, Hamilton, Tarryall, and Breckenridge—before receiving its present name in the late 1880s. Boreas, the Greek god of the north wind, is an appropriate namesake for this gusty mountain route.

The Ute crossed the pass going south to spend their winters in warmer regions. In 1839, Thomas Farnham, a Vermont lawyer, traveled the pass on his trek across Colorado. In the late 1850s, prospectors poured over

RAILROAD WATER TANKS

Depending on the grade and the load, water tanks were typically required at intervals of about thirty miles along a railroad line. They were used to replenish the water carried by the tender—the small car immediately behind the locomotive. The tenders carried coal and about 2,200 gallons of water.

Because of the steep mountain grades between Quartz and the Alpine Tunnel, three tanks were positioned along the tracks. These were originally located at Midway, Woodstock, and Alpine Station.

Tanks were positioned below streams or springs and were gravity-fed. The tank's spout, hinged at the base and upright in its resting position, was lowered onto the tender, and a "flap valve" was opened to fill the tender's tank. The whole operation took about five minutes.

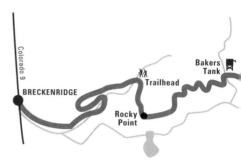

the pass from South Park to reach the gold discoveries in the Blue River district. At this time, the crossing was nothing more than a burro trail, but miners braved the winter snow to walk the pass on snowshoes.

In the 1860s the road was upgraded, and a daily stage traveled across Boreas Pass. In 1884, the Denver, South Park & Pacific Railroad laid narrow-gauge tracks over the pass. For a time, the line was the highest in the United States and required over a dozen

Rotary snowplow clearing the tracks in the winter of 1898

snowsheds. Steep grades of more than 4 percent made the route difficult for trains pulling heavy loads. The grades were such a problem that when P. T. Barnum's circus came to Breckenridge, it had to unload the elephants to help pull the train the last three miles to the summit. The railroad continued to operate until 1937.

In 1952, the U.S. Army Corps of Engineers converted the old railroad grade for automobile use but bypassed the most dangerous section of the route, Windy Point.

Description

This scenic and extremely popular route is suitable for passenger vehicles, although it is unpaved and frequently scarred by numerous potholes.

The route starts in Breckenridge and joins Boreas Pass Road a short distance south of town. Windy Point, identifiable by a large rock outcropping, lies about a half mile from the turnoff onto Boreas Pass Road. The route continues past the restored Bakers Tank.

The summit of Boreas Pass was the site of a Denver, South Park & Pacific Railroad station. The station house, which is being restored as an interpretative center, is only one of the buildings that was located at the site. There was also a two-room telegraph house and a storehouse, as well as a wye in the tracks to allow the trains to turn around.

At Como, the stone roundhouse still stands, but the wooden portion of the roundhouse and the forty-three-room Pacific Hotel were destroyed by fire. The roundhouse is being restored.

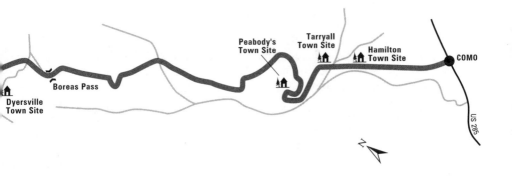

Current Road Conditions

White River National Forest
Dillon Ranger District
680 River Parkway
Silverthorne, CO 80498
(970) 468-5400

Map References

USFS White River NF
      Pike NF
USGS Park County #1
      Summit County #2
Trails Illustrated, #109
The Roads of Colorado, pp. 70–71, 87
Colorado Atlas & Gazetteer, p. 48

Route Directions

▼ 0.0   Outside Breckenridge Visitor
         Information Center at 309 North Main
         Street, zero trip meter and proceed
         south.
21.3 ▲   End at Breckenridge Visitor Information
         Center at 309 North Main Street.
         GPS: N 39°29.12′ W 106°02.73′

▼ 0.8   TL Onto Boreas Pass Road (County 33/
             FR 33).
20.5 ▲   TR Onto Colorado 9.

▼ 4.3   SO Unpaved.
17.0 ▲   SO Paved.

▼ 4.4   SO Cross through gate.
16.9 ▲   SO Cross through gate.

▼ 5.8   SO Walking track on left.

15.5 ▲   SO Walking track on right.

▼ 7.3   SO Bakers Tank on left with walking track
             behind it.
14.0 ▲   SO Bakers Tank on right with walking
             track behind it.

▼ 7.9   SO Track on left.
13.4 ▲   SO Track on right.

▼ 8.2   SO Track on left.
13.1 ▲   SO Track on right.

▼ 9.1   SO Site of Farnham Station, post office,
             and store on left. On right is a walking
             track to Dyersville site, about 0.5 miles
             from road.
12.2 ▲   SO Site of Farnham Station, post office,
             and store on right. On left is a walking
             track to Dyersville site, about 0.5 miles
             from road.
         GPS: N 39°25.50′ W 105°58.88′

▼ 10.6   SO Summit of Boreas Pass and historic
             buildings.
10.7 ▲   SO Summit of Boreas Pass and historic
             buildings.
         GPS: N 39°24.64′ W 105°58.07′

▼ 13.2   SO Cross over Selkirk Gulch Creek.
8.1 ▲   SO Cross over Selkirk Gulch Creek.

▼ 14.4   SO Track on right goes to Upper Tarryall
             Road and access to Selkirk
             Campground.
6.9 ▲   SO Track on left goes to Upper Tarryall Road
             and access to Selkirk Campground.

DENVER, SOUTH PARK & PACIFIC RAILROAD

The Denver, South Park & Pacific Railroad (D,SP&P) was formed in June 1873 by a group led by former Governor John Evans. The initial dream was to operate to Del Norte, then to the San Juan mining district, before proceeding all the way to the West Coast. A lack of funds soon tempered these early dreams.

By 1879, with its house now into order, the tiny Denver, South Park & Pacific Railroad stole a march on two large established railroads. While the Denver & Rio Grande Railroad and the Atchison, Topeka and Santa Fe Railroad were busy fighting a war over access to Royal Gorge, the D,SP&P rapidly laid track toward the boom town of Leadville. It ran track from Denver, across Kenosha Pass to Como, and through to just south of Buena Vista.

However, by the time it got there, the Denver & Rio Grande Railroad had won its battle for Royal Gorge and had the foresight to tie up access along the Arkansas River into Leadville. The D,SP&P was forced to accept the terms it was offered to use the Denver & Rio Grande's rails into Leadville. The only solution for the Denver, South Park & Pacific was to set about building a line across the Continental Divide at Boreas Pass.

This route took it into Breckenridge and then south crossing the Divide for a second time at Climax atop Fremont Pass, as it headed toward Leadville. The financial viability of crossing the Divide twice was aided greatly by the revival of the mining district around Breckenridge—production had increased tenfold from 1879 to 1881. The D,SP&P finally reached Leadville on its own tracks in 1884, four years after the Denver & Rio Grande Railroad.

▼ 15.2 SO Cross over Halfway Gulch Creek.
6.1 ▲ SO Cross over Halfway Gulch Creek.

▼ 17.5 SO Seasonal gate.
3.8 ▲ SO Seasonal gate.

▼ 17.7 SO North Tarryall Creek Road on right.

Boreas Pass railroad snowshed circa 1900

3.6 ▲ SO North Tarryall Creek Road on left.

▼ 18.4 SO Site of Tarryall City mining camp.
2.9 ▲ SO Site of Tarryall City mining camp.

▼ 18.8 SO Cross Tarryall Creek. Mining ruins on right.
2.5 ▲ SO Mining ruins on left. Cross Tarryall Creek.

▼ 20.0 SO Site of Hamilton mining camp.
2.3 ▲ SO Site of Hamilton mining camp.

▼ 20.4 SO Cattle guard. Paved road returns.
0.9 ▲ SO Paved road returns. Cattle guard.

▼ 20.5 SO Town of Como.
0.8 ▲ SO Leaving Como.

▼ 20.7 TL Intersection.
0.6 ▲ TR Intersection.

▼ 20.8 SO Old stone roundhouse on left.
0.5 ▲ SO Old stone roundhouse on right.

▼ 21.3 Cattle guard. End at intersection with US 285.

0.0 ▲ At intersection of Boreas Pass Road (County 33/FR 33) and US 285 in Como, zero trip meter and proceed along County 33 toward Boreas Pass.
GPS: N 39°18.64′ W 105°53.15′

Guanella Pass Trail

The Georgetown railroad loop circa 1900

STARTING POINT Grant, at intersection of US 285 and County 62
FINISHING POINT Georgetown, at Old Georgetown Railway Station
TOTAL MILEAGE 23.4 miles
UNPAVED MILEAGE 11.7 miles
DRIVING TIME 1 hour
ROUTE ELEVATION 8,600 feet to 11,669 feet
USUALLY OPEN Year-round
DIFFICULTY RATING 1
SCENIC RATING 4

Special Attractions

- Attractive scenery with expansive views from the summit.
- An accessible backcountry route, which can be undertaken by passenger vehicles.
- Fall viewing of the aspens.

History

This pass is named for Byron Guanella, a Clear Creek commissioner who was a supporter of building a road over the pass.

Buffalo used to graze their way across this pass, and the Indians used the pass as they followed the migration of the buffalo herds. Early prospectors seeking to use the pass were always on guard against being attacked by the Indians. In 1861, Captain Edward Berthoud and Jim Bridger crossed the pass when surveying potential routes for a railroad west.

The route starts in the town of Grant, which was established in 1870 and originally named Grantville, in honor of President Ulysses S. Grant. Its population peaked at about 200 in 1887.

The route ends in Georgetown, which began as a gold settlement in 1859, when George Griffith from Kentucky found gold there. He brought his brother, their father, George's wife, and a couple of prospectors to the area. They called it George's Town, in honor of George Griffith. The group worked hard to live on the modest amounts of gold they found despite the large amounts of seemingly worthless (at the time) silver-bearing ore in their lode.

In 1864, plentiful veins of quartz were discovered, creating a boom that brought prospectors pouring into the area. The resulting settlement was called Elizabethtown in honor of George's wife, Elizabeth. Before long, George's Town and Elizabethtown combined under the name Georgetown, and a post office was established in 1866.

The following year brought the silver explosion. Houses and businesses were erected at a dizzying rate, the streets buzzed with activity, merchants did brisk business, and lots of people were on the verge of becoming very wealthy. Georgetown was known as the Silver Queen of the Rockies. As it grew, the town acquired an attractive mix of Victorian cottages and a substantial brick business district. Georgetown became the home of many rich men with rich tastes. Large, ornate residences grew in size

Grant in 1938, shortly before the tracks were removed

and ostentation as their owners prospered.

Although Georgetown had a wild side—with more than thirty saloons and plenty of red-light houses and gambling dens—it was also a mining town with culture and refinement. Citizens enjoyed two opera houses, met in public halls and a Masonic lodge, and attended society events. In contrast to most other mining camps, families were an integral part of Georgetown. Schools and churches were constructed from the early days, and homes were built with an air of permanence.

Georgetown is home to many interesting old and historic buildings. The Hotel de Paris (now a museum operated by the National Society of Colonial Dames) was a luxurious French inn of outstanding quality that used to accommodate businessmen from the East and Europe while they speculated over mining investments. President Ulysses S. Grant stayed there and was very fond of it. The Hotel de Paris was richly furnished and served exotic foods. The owners bottled their own wine and kept an extensive wine cellar. Fish were kept in an indoor fountain so they could be selected by and prepared for the guests. The Hammill House (now a museum at Argentine and Third Streets) was once a modest home built by mining investor and politician William A. Hammill. As Hammill grew

wealthier, his house became more opulent. He added bay windows, a solarium with curved glass panels, a stable, an office, and a six-seat outhouse (with three walnut seats for the family and three pine ones for the servants). The Maxwell House is another immaculately kept Victorian home that was quite modest in its original state and took on a much more lavish appearance as the owner prospered.

In 1884, railroad workers accomplished a true feat of engineering when they completed the Georgetown Loop narrow-gauge between Georgetown and Silver Plume (two miles west). A series of curves constructed in a spiral fashion helped trains gain momentum for the steep grades on the straightaways; in one spot, the railroad actually crossed over itself on a three-hundred-foot trestle. The journey, popular with tourists who wanted to observe the beautiful scenery and experience the thrill, was similar to a roller coaster ride.

After the silver crash of 1893, Georgetown became a sleepy mountain town, although it continued to produce gold and other metals. The railroad was abandoned in 1939; the trestle was dismantled, and the rails were scrapped. However, the entire narrow-gauge railway route between Georgetown and Silver Plume has been reconstructed. During Colorado's milder months, thousands of tourists ride the

Georgetown Loop Railroad across the ninety-five-foot Devil's Gate High Bridge between Silver Plume and Georgetown.

Georgetown today is a charming community with interesting architecture and a fascinating history. The town has been a National Historic Landmark since 1966. In 1970, residents formed the Georgetown Society, which has made an ongoing effort to restore and preserve many of Georgetown's Victorian buildings (including the Hammill House) to their original states.

Description

Today, this very popular route is used year-round for picnics, camping, hunting, and cross-country skiing. The easy 2WD route is very scenic and provides good fall viewing of the aspens.

The route starts at the tiny township of Grant and heads north on FR 118 beside Geneva Creek, traveling through a wooded valley with scenic rock formations along the road. The roadside alternates between private property and national forest.

After about four miles, the road starts its climb toward the pass summit and leaves the creek behind. It continues above the timberline, with the scenery becoming considerably more rugged. The summit offers expansive views of Mount Bierstadt, Mount Evans, and the Sawtooth Range to the east and the Continental Divide to the west.

The descent to Georgetown follows Clear Creek past a number of lakes and reservoirs, as well as the Cabin Creek hydroelectric plant.

The route offers access to four U.S. Forest Service campgrounds and numerous hiking trails.

Current Road Conditions

Arapaho and Roosevelt National DForest
Clear Creek Ranger District
101 Chicago Creek Road
Idaho Springs, CO 80452
(303) 567-3000

Map References

USFS   Arapaho and Roosevelt NF
USGS   Clear Creek County
        Park County #2
Trails Illustrated, #104 (most of the route)
The Roads of Colorado, p. 71

Colorado Atlas & Gazetteer, pp. 39, 49

Route Directions

▼ 0.0	At intersection of US 285 and County 62 in Grant, zero trip meter and turn onto Guanella Pass Road toward Georgetown.
12.7 ▲	End at intersection with US 285 in Grant.
	GPS: N 39°27.61′ W 105°39.75′

| ▼ 0.5 | SO | Unpaved. |
| 12.2 ▲ | SO | Paved. |

| ▼ 1.3 | SO | Enter National Forest. |
| 11.4 ▲ | SO | Leave National Forest. |

| ▼ 1.6 | SO | Geneva Creek Picnic Grounds. |
| 11.1 ▲ | SO | Geneva Creek Picnic Grounds. |

| ▼ 2.3 | SO | USFS Whiteside Campground. |
| 10.4 ▲ | SO | USFS Whiteside Campground. |

| ▼ 2.7 | SO | Driving through Geneva Creek Canyon. |
| 10.0 ▲ | SO | Driving through Geneva Creek Canyon. |

| ▼ 5.0 | SO | Cattle guard. |
| 7.7 ▲ | SO | Cattle guard. |

| ▼ 5.1 | SO | Geneva Park. |
| 7.6 ▲ | SO | Geneva Park. |

| ▼ 5.2 | SO | USFS Burning Bear Campground. |
| 7.5 ▲ | SO | USFS Burning Bear Campground. |

| ▼ 6.0 | SO | Track to Geneva City town site at Duck Creek Picnic Ground on left. |
| 6.7 ▲ | SO | Track to Geneva City town site at Duck Creek Picnic Ground on right. |

| ▼ 6.7 | SO | Track on left to Geneva Creek (FR 119). |
| 6.0 ▲ | SO | Track on right to Geneva Creek (FR 119). |

| ▼ 9.2 | SO | Unpaved. |
| 3.5 ▲ | SO | Paved. |

| ▼ 12.7 | SO | Summit of Guanella Pass. Zero trip meter. |

NC Trail #13: Guanella Pass Trail

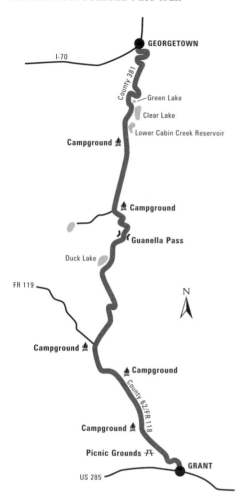

0.0 ▲   Continue toward Grant.

      GPS: N 39°35.72' W 105°42.61'

▼ 0.0   Continue toward Georgetown.
10.7 ▲   SO   Summit of Guanella Pass. Zero trip meter.

▼ 1.8   SO   Silver Dollar Lake Trail (1 mile) on left.
8.9 ▲   SO   Silver Dollar Lake Trail (1 mile) on right.

▼ 1.9   SO   USFS Guanella Campground on left.
8.8 ▲   SO   USFS Guanella Campground on right.

▼ 3.7   SO   Cross over South Clear Creek.
7.0 ▲   SO   Cross over South Clear Creek.

▼ 4.7   SO   USFS Clear Lake Campground on left.
6.0 ▲   SO   USFS Clear Lake Campground on right.

▼ 4.8   SO   Paved.
5.9 ▲   SO   Unpaved.

▼ 6.0   SO   Clear Lake on right.
4.7 ▲   SO   Clear Lake on left.

▼ 6.5   SO   Green Lake on right.
4.2 ▲   SO   Green Lake on left.

▼ 7.7   SO   Road on left to Waldorf and Argentine Pass.
3.0 ▲   SO   Road on right to Waldorf and Argentine Pass.

▼ 8.5   SO   Georgetown reservoir on right.
2.2 ▲   SO   Georgetown reservoir on left.

▼ 10.0   SO   Enter Georgetown, remaining on the paved road. As it comes into town, the name becomes Rose Street.
0.7 ▲   SO   Leave Georgetown on Rose Street toward Guanella Pass.

▼ 10.7   End at Georgetown Loop Railroad station on the corner of Rose and 11th Streets.
0.0 ▲   From the Georgetown Loop Railroad station at the corner of Rose and 11th Streets in Georgetown, zero trip meter and proceed south along Rose Street, which will become County 381.

      GPS: N 39°42.69' W 105°41.69'

Shrine Pass Trail

STARTING POINT Redcliff
FINISHING POINT Interstate 70, at exit 190 near Vail Pass
TOTAL MILEAGE 10.8 miles
UNPAVED MILEAGE 10.7 miles
DRIVING TIME 3/4 hour
ROUTE ELEVATION 8,800 to 11,089 feet

Redcliff circa 1915

USUALLY OPEN Mid-June to late September
DIFFICULTY RATING 2
SCENIC RATING 8

Special Attractions
■ Spectacular views of the Mount of the Holy Cross.
■ Fall viewing of the aspens.
■ Summer wildflowers.

History
Shrine Pass is so named because it overlooks and provides a wonderful view of the Mount of the Holy Cross, a famous fourteen-thousand-foot peak. The route was an Indian trail. It rose to prominence in the 1920s when Orion W. Draggett, a Redcliff newspaper publisher, proposed a shrine be built there. His amazing plans included not only viewing facilities but also an airport and a golf course. In 1931, he opened the road that he intended to use for this project, attracting a crowd of hundreds to the event. The project was never undertaken, but proponents continued to raise it periodically for some years. Before 1940, the pass road served as the main route between Denver and Grand Junction.

The Mount of the Holy Cross was declared a national monument by President Herbert Hoover; but it lost its status in 1950 due to the deterioration of the right arm of the cross.

Description
The route leaves Redcliff and travels initially beside Turkey Creek through the narrow, wooded valley. As the route gains altitude, there are a number of viewing spots along the way that provide distant but spectacular

NC Trail #14: Shrine Pass Trail

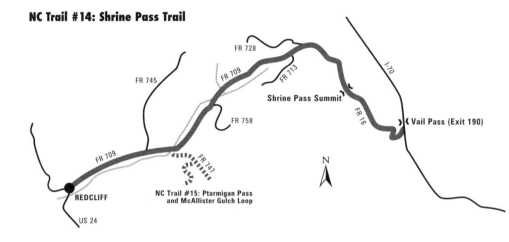

views of the Mount of the Holy Cross to the southwest. Closer to the broad, open pass, are alpine meadows that are famous for their vivid wildflower displays in summer. The huge stands of aspens also attract many sightseers in the fall. In the winter, the area is very popular for cross-country skiing.

The road is easy and accessible to 2WD vehicles the entire distance.

Current Road Conditions
White River National Forest
Holy Cross Ranger District
24747 US Hwy 24, Minturn, CO 81645
(970) 827-5715

Map References
USFS White River NF
USGS Summit County #2
        Eagle County #4
Trails Illustrated, #108
The Roads of Colorado, p. 70
Colorado Atlas & Gazetteer, pp. 37–38

Route Directions

▼ 0.0		At intersection of US 24 and FR 709 in Redcliff, zero trip meter and proceed east, following sign to Shrine Pass (FR 709).
2.4 ▲		End at intersection with US 24 in Redcliff.
		GPS: N 39°30.78′ W 106°22.03′

▼ 0.1   SO Unpaved.

2.3 ▲	SO	Paved.

▼ 1.9	SO	Seasonal gate. FR 745 on left.
0.5 ▲	SO	FR 745 on right. Seasonal gate.

▼ 2.4	SO	Track on right over bridge is North-Central #15: Ptarmigan Pass and McAllister Gulch Loop. Zero trip meter.
0.0 ▲		Continue along FR 709 toward Redcliff.
		GPS: N 39°31.39′ W 106°19.49′

▼ 0.0		Continue along FR 709 toward Shrine Pass.
8.4 ▲	SO	Track on left over bridge is North-Central #15: Ptarmigan Pass and McAllister Gulch Loop. Zero trip meter.

▼ 0.6	SO	FR 258 on right. Cabins.
7.8 ▲	SO	Cabins. FR 258 on left.

▼ 1.7	SO	Cross over Turkey Creek.
6.7 ▲	SO	Cross over Turkey Creek.

▼ 3.2	SO	Cross over creek.
5.2 ▲	SO	Cross over creek.

▼ 3.4	SO	Track on right.
5.0 ▲	SO	Track on left.

▼ 4.0	TL	FR 713 on right.
4.4 ▲	TR	FR 713 on left.
		GPS: N 39°33.41′ W 106°16.07′

▼ 4.7   BR FR 728 on left.

3.7 ▲	BL	FR 728 on right.
▼ 5.3	SO	Track on right.
3.1 ▲	SO	Track on left.
▼ 6.2	SO	Summit of Shrine Pass. Track on right.
2.2 ▲	SO	Track on left. Summit of Shrine Pass.
		GPS: N 39°32.72′ W 106°14.45′
▼ 8.4		Seasonal gate, then in 100 yards, a stop sign. Paved road. End at interstate 70.
0.0 ▲		The intersection for Shrine Pass is on I-70 at exit 190, approximately 1 mile east of Vail Pass summit. Zero trip meter where the side road goes from paved to unpaved.
		GPS: N 39°31.74′ W 106°13.06′

Ptarmigan Pass and McAllister Gulch Loop

STARTING POINT Intersection of North-Central #14: Shrine Pass Trail (FR 709) and FR 747

FINISHING POINT Intersection of North-Central #14: Shrine Pass Trail (FR 709) and FR 747

TOTAL MILEAGE 21.4 miles

UNPAVED MILEAGE 21.4 miles

DRIVING TIME 3 hours

ROUTE ELEVATION 9,200 feet to 11,765 feet

USUALLY OPEN Mid-June to late September

DIFFICULTY RATING 4

SCENIC RATING 9

Special Attractions

- Panoramic views of the Mount of the Holy Cross, a fourteen-thousand-foot peak.
- Numerous creek crossings.
- Historic site of the Camp Hale Army Base.
- Interesting loop route that is only moderately difficult.

History

During World War II, this area was used as a training ground for the Tenth Mountain Division of the U.S. Army, based at the now decommissioned Camp Hale Army Base. The base was the only facility that offered training in mountain and winter warfare. The division fought with distinction, and after the war, a number of the veterans from the Tenth Mountain Division were instrumental in establishing Colorado's ski industry.

Description

This route is a side road of North-Central #14: Shrine Pass Trail. Initially, it travels through a very scenic, narrow canyon with barely enough room at its base for the road and Wearyman Creek. The road crosses through the shallow creek a number of times before reaching FR 708 in less than a mile.

FR 708 immediately starts to climb steeply and continues through the dense forest with numerous switchbacks, where passing oncoming vehicles is possible. The road rises above timberline into a broad alpine meadow and continues to the top of Hornsilver Mountain, from which point there is a spectacular 360-degree view; to the southwest is the Holy Cross Wilderness Area and the Mount of the Holy Cross, a famous fourteen-thousand-foot peak. This mountain was declared a national monument by President Herbert Hoover; but it lost its status in 1950 due to the deterioration of the right arm of the cross.

The route continues across a fairly level ridge to Resolution Mountain. At around the six-mile point, the road commences a steep descent for about half a mile. As you

Camp Hale Army Base in the 1940s

A section of trail typical of this route

turn onto FR 702 (Resolution Road), a right turn takes you to the old Camp Hale Army Base and US 24. The route continues to the left toward Ptarmigan Pass. The road to the pass is wide and well maintained.

The descent from the pass via FR 747 (Wearyman Road) heads back below timberline and is rough, narrow, and often boggy. There is also another short section of shelf road. You will have to cross the creek several times before returning to the intersection with Shrine Pass Road.

We highly recommend the *Trails Illustrated* maps listed below to assist with navigation of this route.

Current Road Conditions
White River National Forest
Holy Cross Ranger District
24747 US Hwy 24, Minturn, CO 81645
(970) 827-5715

Map References
USFS   White River NF
USGS   Eagle County #4
           Summit County #2

Trails Illustrated, #108, #109
The Roads of Colorado, p. 70
Colorado Atlas & Gazetteer, pp. 37, 47

Route Directions

▼ 0.0   From intersection of North-Central #14: Shrine Pass Trail (FR 709) and FR 747, zero trip meter at Wearyman Creek bridge and proceed toward Ptarmigan Pass and McAllister Gulch.
0.7 ▲   Cross bridge and end at North-Central #14: Shrine Pass Trail (FR 709).
         GPS: N 39°31.39' W 106°19.49'

▼ 0.2   SO   Cross through creek; then 100 yards farther, cross through creek again.
0.5 ▲   SO   Cross through creek; then 100 yards farther, cross through creek again.

▼ 0.3   SO   Cross through creek.
0.4 ▲   SO   Cross through creek.

▼ 0.4   SO   Cross through creek.
0.3 ▲   SO   Cross through creek.

▼ 0.7   TR   Cross through creek. Intersection with McAllister Gulch Road (FR 708). Zero trip meter.
0.0 ▲   Proceed along FR 747.
         GPS: N 39°31.20' W 106°18.87'

▼ 0.0   Proceed along FR 708.
10.0 ▲   TL   Intersection with Wearyman Road (FR 747) Cross through creek. Zero trip meter.

▼ 1.1   BR   Fork in road.
8.9 ▲   BL   Fork in road.

▼ 2.1   BL   Track on right.
7.9 ▲   BR   Track on left.

▼ 2.2   BL   Track on right.
7.8 ▲   BR   Track on left.

▼ 2.9   BL   Intersection. Spot on right with broad, panoramic views of Eagle River Valley to the southwest and northwest.
7.0 ▲   BR   Intersection. Spot on left with broad,

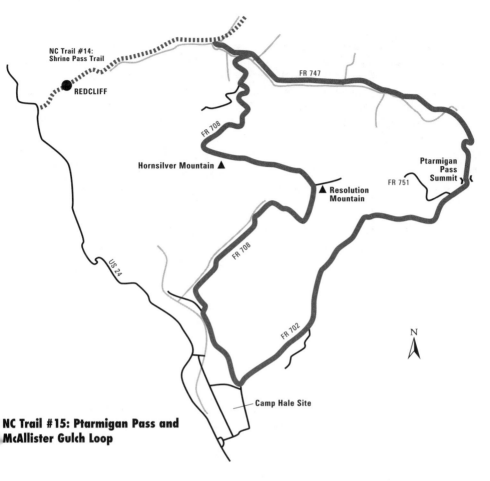

NC Trail #14:
Shrine Pass Trail

FR 747

REDCLIFF

FR 708

Hornsilver Mountain ▲

▲ Resolution
Mountain

FR 751

Ptarmigan
Pass
Summit

US 24

FR 708

FR 702

N

Camp Hale Site

NC Trail #15: Ptarmigan Pass and
McAllister Gulch Loop

panoramic views of Eagle River Valley
to the southwest and northwest.
GPS: N 39°29.98' W 106°19.88'

▼ 3.6 SO Meadow at top of Hornsilver Mountain
with 360-degree views.
6.4 ▲ SO Meadow at top of Hornsilver Mountain
with 360-degree views.
GPS: N 39°29.86' W 106°19.41'

▼ 4.3 BR Intersection.
5.6 ▲ BL Intersection.
GPS: N 39°29.27' W 106°17.82'

▼ 8.4 SO Private cabin on right. National Forest
boundary.
1.6 ▲ SO National Forest boundary. Private cabin
on left.

▼ 8.8 TL Intersection. Track on right dead-ends.

1.2 ▲ TR Intersection. Sign to McAllister Gulch.
Dead end is straight ahead.
GPS: N 39°27.76' W 106°19.76'

▼ 9.2 TL Intersection. Follow Ptarmigan Pass
sign to the left.
0.8 ▲ TR Intersection.

▼ 10.0 TL Intersection with Resolution Road (FR
702). Road on right connects with US
24 in 1.1 miles and site of old Camp
Hale U.S. Army Base. Zero trip meter.
0.0 ▲ Continue along FR 708.
GPS: N 39°26.90' W 106°19.12'

▼ 0.0 Continue along FR 702.
5.3 ▲ TR Onto FR 708. Zero trip meter

▼ 0.2 SO Seasonal gate.

5.1 ▲	SO	Seasonal gate.

▼ 1.3	SO	Track on right dead-ends. Remain on Resolution Road (FR 702).
4.0 ▲	SO	Track on left dead-ends.

▼ 4.8	TR	Intersection with FR 751.
0.5 ▲	TL	Intersection with Resolution Road (FR 702)

▼ 5.3	SO	Summit of Ptarmigan Pass. Road becomes FR 747. Zero trip meter.
0.0 ▲		Continue along FR 702.
		GPS: N 39°29.59′ W 106°15.14′

▼ 0.0		Continue along FR 747.
5.4 ▲	SO	Summit of Ptarmigan Pass. Road becomes FR 702. Zero trip meter.

▼ 1.4	SO	Cross through creek.
4.0 ▲	SO	Cross through creek.

▼ 2.1	SO	Cross through creek.
3.2 ▲	SO	Cross through creek.

▼ 3.1	SO	Cross through creek.
2.3 ▲	SO	Cross through creek.

▼ 4.6	SO	Cross through creek.
0.8 ▲	SO	Cross through creek.

▼ 4.7	SO	Intersection with FR 708 to McAllister Gulch on left. Cross through creek.
0.7 ▲	SO	Cross through creek. Intersection with FR 708 to McAllister Gulch on right.
		GPS: N 39°31.20′ W 106°18.87′

▼ 5.0	SO	Cross through creek.
0.4 ▲	SO	Cross through creek.

▼ 5.1	SO	Cross through creek.
0.3 ▲	SO	Cross through creek.

▼ 5.2	SO	Cross through creek.
0.2 ▲	SO	Cross through creek.

▼ 5.3	SO	Cross through creek.
0.1 ▲	SO	Cross through creek.

▼ 5.4		Cross bridge and end at Shrine Pass

Trail (FR 709).

0.0 ▲		From intersection of North-Central #14: Shrine Pass Trail (FR 709) and FR 747, zero trip meter at Wearyman Creek bridge and proceed toward Ptarmigan Pass and McAllister Gulch.
		GPS: N 39°31.39′ W 106°19.49′

Weston Pass Trail

STARTING POINT Intersection of US 24 and County 7, 5.1 miles south of Leadville Airport

FINISHING POINT Intersection of Park County 5 and US 285

TOTAL MILEAGE 25.7 miles

UNPAVED MILEAGE 23.4 miles

DRIVING TIME 1 1/2 hours

ROUTE ELEVATION 9,400 feet to 11,921 feet

USUALLY OPEN Late June to late September

DIFFICULTY RATING 2

SCENIC RATING 7

Special Attractions

- Attractive scenery along an easy 4WD trail.
- Access to a network of 4WD trails.

History

Like so many passes in the Colorado Rockies, Weston Pass was a Ute trail before being developed as a wagon road. In 1860, during the first gold boom in the Leadville area, the new wagon road was known as the Ute Trail. The stagecoach way station on the eastern side of the pass grew into the town of Weston. Father Dyer made early use of the pass and in 1861 was caught in a blizzard and nearly perished.

Four freight and passenger service companies sprang up to meet the enormous demand. One, the Wall & Witter Stage Company, maintained four hundred horses, eleven freight wagons, and seven stagecoaches to service its operations. In 1873, the Hayden survey party found a good wagon road over Weston Pass at a time

A view of one of the stands of aspens along the Weston Pass route

when there was barely a burro trail over Mosquito Pass.

The Denver, South Park & Pacific Railroad reached Weston in 1879, adding new impetus to the town's growth. In that year, the Wall & Witter Stage Company collected $1.5 million in fares; on just one day in September, 225 teams were counted as they crossed the pass, pulling either wagons or stagecoaches. As proof that traveling the pass road was thirsty work, Park County issued no fewer than eight new liquor licenses in 1879 to establishments between the town and the top of the pass.

However, in 1881, the railroad made it into Leadville, sending Weston Pass into rapid decline.

In the 1950s, the pass road was renovated and has been well maintained ever since as a recreational road.

Description

The route commences at the intersection of US 24 and County 7, 5.1 miles south of the Leadville Airport entrance on the left as you leave Leadville.

Navigation along the Weston Pass route is a simple matter, and the road is suitable for cars—except for a couple of miles on the west side of the summit, where high clearance is preferable.

The road travels beside Union Creek on the west side and along the South Fork of the South Platte River on the east side. Both offer numerous, good backcountry camping sites. Additionally, on the west side there is a U.S. Forest Service campground.

Current Road Conditions

Pike National Forest
Leadville Ranger District
810 Front Street, Leadville, CO 80461
(719) 486-0749

Map References

USFS   Pike NF
            San Isabel NF
USGS   Park County #3
            Lake County
Trails Illustrated, #110
The Roads of Colorado, p. 86
Colorado Atlas & Gazetteer, pp. 47–48

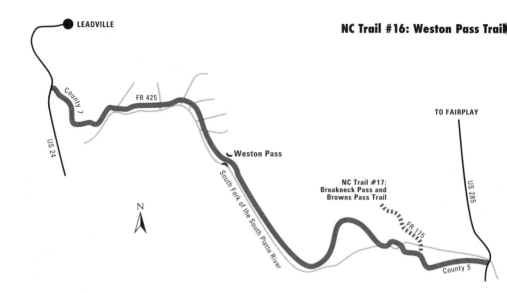

Route Directions

▼ 0.0   At intersection of US 24 and County 7, zero trip meter and proceed southeast along County 7 (FR 425) toward Weston Pass. There is a sign for Massive Lakes.

10.5 ▲   End at intersection with US 24.
GPS: N 39°10.58′ W 106°19.27′

▼ 3.0 SO Cattle guard.
7.5 ▲ SO Cattle guard.

▼ 7.1 SO Cross over creek.
3.4 ▲ SO Cross over creek.

▼ 7.5 SO Track on left.
3.0 ▲ SO Track on right.

▼ 8.4 SO Track on left.
2.1 ▲ SO Track on right.

▼ 8.7 SO Cabin ruins on right.
1.8 ▲ SO Cabin ruins on left.

▼ 8.8 SO Track on left.
1.7 ▲ SO Track on right.

▼ 9.3 SO Cabin ruins below shelf road.
1.2 ▲ SO Cabin ruins below shelf road.

▼ 10.4 SO Track on right.
0.1 ▲ SO Track on left.

▼ 10.5 SO Summit of Weston Pass. Zero trip meter.
0.0 ▲ Continue along FR 425.
GPS: N 39°07.88′ W 106°10.88′

▼ 0.0 Continue along FR 425.
8.4 ▲ SO Summit of Weston Pass. Zero trip meter.

▼ 0.1 SO Cabin ruins on the left and right. Track on left to small lake.
8.3 ▲ SO Track on right to small lake. Cabin ruins on the left and right.

▼ 0.2 SO Site of the Ruby Mine.
8.2 ▲ SO Site of the Ruby Mine.

▼ 0.8 SO Track on left.
7.6 ▲ SO Track on right.

▼ 1.7 SO Track on left.
6.7 ▲ SO Track on right.

▼ 1.9 SO Site of Park Place roadside restaurant on left.
6.5   SO Site of Park Place roadside restaurant on right.

▼ 4.5   SO Road on right to USFS Weston Pass
            Campground.
3.9 ▲   SO Road on left to USFS Weston Pass
            Campground.
            GPS: N 39°04.63′ W 106°07.99′

▼ 5.6   SO Rich Creek Trailhead on right and cattle
            guard. Leave the National Forest.
2.8 ▲   SO Leave the National Forest. Cattle
            guard, then Rich Creek Trailhead on
            left.

▼ 6.8   BL Road on right goes to a private ranch.
1.6 ▲   CR Road on left goes to a private ranch.

▼ 7.5   SO Cattle guard.
0.9 ▲   SO Cattle guard.

▼ 7.9   SO Road on left.
0.5 ▲   SO Road on right.

▼ 8.4   TL FR 425 ends at fork in the road. Left
            fork goes to US 285 via County 5.
            Right fork goes to US 285 via County
            22. Both alternatives reach the high-

way in seven miles. Zero trip meter.
0.0 ▲   Proceed along FR 425.
        GPS: N 39°05.85′ W 106°05.28′

▼ 0.0   Proceed along County 5.
6.8 ▲   BR Onto FR 425. Zero trip meter.

▼ 1.6   SO Cattle guard.
5.2 ▲   SO Cattle guard.

▼ 1.9   BR Road on left.
4.9 ▲   BL Road on right.

▼ 2.2   SO Cattle guard.
4.6 ▲   SO Cattle guard.

▼ 3.6   SO Cattle guard.
3.2 ▲   SO Cattle guard.

▼ 5.2   SO North-Central #17: Breakneck Pass
            and Browns Pass Trail on left. Cattle
            guard.
1.6 ▲   SO Cattle guard. North-Central #17:
            Breakneck Pass and Brown Pass Trail
            on right.

A section of trail typical of this route

▼ 6.8   Cattle guard, then end at intersection with US 285.

0.0 ▲   At intersection of US 285 and Park County 5, zero trip meter and proceed west on Weston Pass Road, County 5. Cross cattle grid and follow sign to Weston Pass.
         GPS: N 39°09.20' W 105°59.93'

NORTH-CENTRAL REGION TRAIL #17

Breakneck Pass and Browns Pass Trail

STARTING POINT Intersection of US 285 and Park County 5
FINISHING POINT Intersection of County 20 and US 285
TOTAL MILEAGE 13.9 miles
UNPAVED MILEAGE 11.8 miles
DRIVING TIME 1 1/2 hours
ROUTE ELEVATION 9,600 feet to 11,372 feet
USUALLY OPEN Early June to early October
DIFFICULTY RATING 3
SCENIC RATING 7

Special Attractions
■ Access to a network of 4WD trails.
■ Fairly easy 4WD trail that travels under the canopy of the dense forest.
■ Aspen viewing in the fall.

History
Little is known about the history of these two pass roads; but it is likely that they were built, or at least improved, in the early 1900s to open access to the mines in the Sheep Park area.

Description
The route commences at the intersection of US 285 and North-Central #16: Weston Pass Trail (County 5) about 4.5 miles south of Fairplay and travels through attractive ranch land for 1.6 miles before turning onto

Breakneck Pass Road (FR 175).

Proceeding from the intersection, the road is fairly steep and rocky in sections. It might also be boggy if it has rained recently. The clearance between the trees is tight in spots, especially for full-sized vehicles. Nonetheless, although the road becomes rough and narrow, it is not difficult.

The unmarked Breakneck Pass is at the intersection with FR 426, at which point the main road proceeds straight on, the road on the left is closed, and FR 426 (to the right) takes you on an alternative loop past ruins of a mine and a cabin. FR 426 is a more interesting route than FR 175 from this point and rejoins the main road at the start of Sheep Park. The route directions for FR 426 are provided below.

As you travel through Sheep Park, Browns Pass Road (FR 176) turns off to the right. The track climbs uphill steeply for about three-tenths of a mile and can be quite difficult if it is wet (under which circumstances the road's difficulty rating would be higher than 3). After this initial ascent, the road levels out and is easy except for some tight clearance between the trees. Browns Pass is marked with a rough sign.

This little-used route lacks the drama of many 4WD roads in Colorado but offers a variety of scenery from the tranquil meadows of Sheep Park to dense forests with thick stands of aspen that cover the road in gold during the fall. Some higher sections of the route also provide good views of the Mosquito Range to the west.

Current Road Conditions
Pike National Forest
South Park Ranger District
320 Hwy 285, Fairplay, CO 80440
(719) 836-2031

Map References
USFS Pike NF
USGS Park County #1
         Park County #3
Trails Illustrated, #110
The Roads of Colorado, p. 86
Colorado Atlas & Gazetteer, p. 48

The remains of a miner's cabin near Breakneck Pass

Route Directions

▼ 0.0   At intersection of US 285 and Park County 5, zero trip meter and proceed west on Weston Pass Road, County 5. Cross cattle grid and follow sign to Weston Pass.

5.0 ▲   End at intersection with US 285.
GPS: N 39°09.20' W 105°59.93'

▼ 1.6   TR   Cross cattle guard. Turn onto Breakneck Pass Road (FR 175).

3.4 ▲   TL   Turn onto County 5. Cross cattle guard.
GPS: N 39°08.39' W 106°01.42'

▼ 3.2   SO   Cattle guard. Enter Pike National Forest.

1.8 ▲   SO   Leave Pike National Forest. Cattle guard.

▼ 3.5   SO   Track on left to camping.

1.5 ▲   SO   Track on right to camping.

▼ 5.0   TR   Intersection with Round Hill Road (FR 426) on right. To the left, FR 426 is closed a little farther on. Zero trip meter.

0.0 ▲   Continue along FR 175.
GPS: N 39°08.91' W 106°04.65'

▼ 0.0   Proceed along FR 426.

2.8 ▲   TL   Intersection with Breakneck Pass Road (FR 175). Zero trip meter.

▼ 1.4   BL   Track on right. Cabin ruins and mine.

1.4 ▲   BR   Track on left. Cabin ruins and mine.

▼ 1.6   SO   Cabin ruins on right.

1.2 ▲   SO   Cabin ruins on left.

▼ 2.0   TR   Intersection to rejoin FR 175.

0.8 ▲   TL   Intersection with FR 426, a faint trail to the left near the end of Sheep Park.

▼ 2.8   BR   Onto Browns Pass Road (FR 176). Zero trip meter.

0.0 ▲   Proceed along FR 175.
GPS: N 39°10.35' W 106°06.42'

▼ 0.0   Proceed along FR 176.

6.1 ▲   BL   Onto FR 175. Zero trip meter.

▼ 0.5   SO   Several cabin ruins on right.

5.6 ▲   SO   Several cabin ruins on left.

▼ 0.6   SO   Summit of Browns Pass. FR 1761 track on the left.

5.5 ▲   SO   Summit of Browns Pass. FR 1761 track on the right.
GPS: N 39°10.47' W 106°05.77'

NC Trail #17: Breakness Pass and Browns Pass Trail

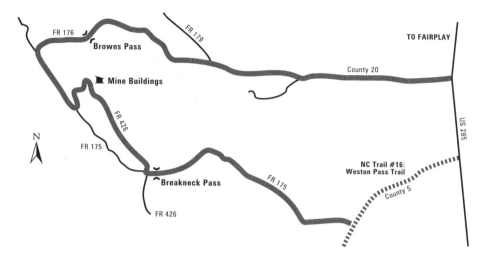

FR 176
Browns Pass
FR 179
TO FAIRPLAY
County 20
Mine Buildings
FR 426
N
FR 175
NC Trail #16:
Weston Pass Trail
Breakneck Pass
FR 175
County 5
US 285
FR 426

▼ 1.1   SO   Cabin ruins on right.
5.0 ▲   SO   Cabin ruins on left.

▼ 1.4   BR   Track on left.
4.7 ▲   BL   Track on right.

▼ 2.8   SO   Cross through creek.
3.3 ▲   SO   Cross through creek.

▼ 2.9   BR   Track on left (FR 179). Remain on
FR 176.

A stand of aspens envelops the road near Breakneck Pass

3.2 ▲   BL   Track on right (FR 179). Remain on
FR 176.
GPS: N 39°10.17′ W 106°03.53′

▼ 3.2   SO   FR 178 on left.
2.9 ▲   SO   FR 178 on right.

▼ 3.4   SO   Leaving Pike National Forest. Gate
(leave it as you find it).
2.7 ▲   SO   Gate (leave it as you find it). Entering
Pike National Forest.

▼ 3.6   SO   Gravel road.
2.5 ▲   SO   Gravel road.

▼ 4.0   TL   Intersection with County 20.
2.1 ▲   TR   Turn from County 20 onto FR 176.
Signs read: "Browns Pass, Fourmile
Road, National Forest Access."
GPS: N 39°09.99′ W 106°02.45′

▼ 4.5   SO   Cattle guard.
1.6 ▲   SO   Cattle guard.

▼ 6.1   Cattle guard. End at intersection with
US 285.
0.0 ▲   At intersection of County 20 and US
285 (there is a sign for National Forest
access and Browns Pass), zero trip
meter and proceed along County 20.
GPS: N 39°10.14′ W 106°00.06′

Mosquito Pass Trail

STARTING POINT Colorado 9 and Mosquito Pass
Road (Park County 12) at Alma
Junction

FINISHING POINT Leadville

TOTAL MILEAGE 16.7 miles

UNPAVED MILEAGE 15.2 miles

DRIVING TIME 2 hours

ROUTE ELEVATION 10,200 feet to 13,186 feet

USUALLY OPEN Early August to mid-September

DIFFICULTY RATING 4

SCENIC RATING 9

Special Attractions

■ The highest pass road in America.
■ Great historic significance.
■ Wonderful alpine views.

History

According to legend, this pass got its name
in 1861 at a meeting of local residents who
gathered to try to choose one of the many
names proposed at their previous, inconclu-
sive meeting. When they opened the min-

utes from that meeting, they found that a
mosquito had been squashed in the middle
of their list of proposed names. The new
name was approved by acclamation!

The Indians used the pass, but the first
white men recorded to have crossed it were
Thomas Farnham and his party in their
exploratory journey across Colorado in
1839. In 1861, the Mosquito gold-mining
camp was established to the east of the pass.

From 1864, the pass was used by the itinerant Methodist preacher Father Dyer, who
carried the mail across the pass for pay of
eighteen dollars per week. In winter, he traveled on snowshoes at night when the surface
of the snow was harder. A small memorial to
him stands at the summit of the pass.

Horace A. W. Tabor crossed the pass with
Augusta, his wife, on horseback in 1870 but
noted that a road barely existed. In 1873,
Hayden's survey team crossed the pass and
noted only a well-used burro trail.

Western Union built a telegraph line over
the pass in 1878. Later that year, Horace
Tabor and other investors formed the
Mosquito Pass Wagon Road Company to
construct a toll road over the pass. This
wagon road was completed the following

A view of the trail on the east side approach to Mosquito Pass

LEADVILLE

As early as 1860, prospectors staked claims in California Gulch, which yielded gold for the following six years. The camp was then called Oro City. Miner H. A. W. (Horace) Tabor, along with his wife, Augusta, arrived during a food shortage. By sacrificing his oxen to feed the miners, Tabor made many friends.

The gold soon played out but was followed by rich discoveries of silver. In 1877, the area's silver boom began, and the town began to evolve. Hundreds of prospectors arrived daily and slept wherever they could. Some slept in alleyways, some in tents, and one saloon even rented out floor space (the owner is said to have saved the tabletops for regular customers). Still, others could not find room in the saloons, and hundreds died of exposure.

Officially named Leadville in January 1878, the town was incorporated the following month. Later that year, two prospectors asked Tabor to lend them seventeen dollars' worth of mining supplies in exchange for a one-third interest in their findings. The two prospectors discovered a mine about a mile up East 7th Street, which they called the Little Pittsburg. It turned out to be one of the richest silver lodes in Colorado and promptly made all three men millionaires. Tabor became Leadville's first mayor that same year.

By the summer of 1879, Leadville's architects and builders had endowed the town with a sophisticated air. The town was quickly blossoming with nineteen hotels, eighty-two saloons, thirty-eight restaurants, thirteen liquor houses, ten lumber yards, seven smelting and reductions works, two works for ore testing, twelve blacksmith shops, six jewelry stores, three undertakers, twenty-one gambling houses, and thirty-six brothels. The town grew so prosperous that not only miners but also merchants, business owners, and artisans could earn a comfortable living.

Leadville became a place where countless fortunes could be made. Even seemingly barren mines produced. Leadville claimed that in a ten-year period it had created more millionaires than any city in the world. And there were many places for rich men to spend their money. The red-light district along State Street was a notorious haunt for the most infamous of Leadville's early gamblers. It was considered to be one of the most wicked and rowdy areas in the entire West. Easy money inevitably encouraged lawlessness. Violence, murder, and thievery were prevalent in Leadville. Anyone who flashed a wad of cash could be staked out as prey. It was dangerous to walk the streets at night.

Leadville saw some interesting characters and fortunes come and go. Doc Holliday had a famed dispute with a Leadville bartender. The bartender, who had previously lent Holliday five dollars, demanded to be repaid. He followed Holliday into a saloon and threatened to "lick" him if he did not get his money back right away. Holliday drew his pistol and fired a shot that wounded the bartender in his arm. Holliday was taken into custody, tried, and acquitted. "Broken Nose Scotty" sold his mining

Leadville in its early days

claim for $30,000 while he was in jail for drunkenness. With the proceeds he paid bail for all the other inmates, bought everyone new clothes, and then took them out on the town. Needless to say, before the night was over the group was back in jail for disturbing the peace! Once, a group of men were digging a grave for their friend when they struck a fortune. Their poor "friend" ended up buried in a snowbank. Young Margaret Tobin was nineteen years old when she married J. J. Brown. After Brown struck it rich on the Little Jonny Mine, the couple moved to Denver. Mrs. Brown later became famous as a survivor of the Titanic and was subsequently known as the Unsinkable Molly Brown.

During its boom years, Leadville's population swelled to somewhere between twenty and forty thousand. It was the second largest city in Colorado. The Tabor Opera House (310 Harrison Avenue) was opened in 1879 with the financial assistance of Horace Tabor. The Great Houdini, poet Oscar Wilde, and John Philip Sousa's Marine Band are among the famous performers who made appearances there. (It is rumored that Wilde drank the miners under the table at local saloons.) Tabor was also responsible for construction of the Tabor Grand Hotel, which opened in 1885. Its famous lobby floor was imbedded with silver dollars, and its bar was known as the best-stocked bar in the state. (Renamed the Hotel Vendome in 1894, it still stands at 701 Harrison Avenue.)

Tabor and his wife began to drift apart. A woman of simple taste, Augusta frowned on her husband's free spending and did not enjoy the lavish life the two led after striking it rich. In 1881, Tabor met and romanced beautiful divorcee Elizabeth McCourt Doe (Baby Doe). Their relationship became an open secret, and Tabor and Augusta were divorced the following year. Tabor and Baby Doe were married in an elaborate wedding in Washington, D.C., in 1883.

Ten years later Tabor lost everything in the silver crash, as all his money was tied up in silver investments. Baby Doe remained a devoted wife as Tabor was forced to sell everything—except the Matchless Mine (two miles east on 7th Street), which Tabor strongly believed would once again become valuable. After Tabor's death in 1899, Baby Doe moved into a small shack on the premises. She became a recluse and destitute. Thirty-six years later, in March 1935, her lifeless body, clad in rags, frozen in the shape of a cross, was found in the cabin next to the mine. Surrounding her were scrapbooks with yellowed pages and mementos of the elegant life she had once known.

After the turn of the century, Leadville's economy was in shambles. Mine production had dropped to a fraction of what it had been, and houses were torn down for firewood. Leadville became a source of illicit whiskey, the county's major source of income during prohibition. Today Leadville is home to a few thousand residents, but it never did revive. Although it is not an especially pretty town, with a little imagination one can still glimpse the faded splendor of a long-gone era.

ear, when freight wagons and stagecoaches were among the 150 vehicles crossing the pass each day. The pass became known as the "highway of frozen death" because of the many travelers who froze to death while walking across the pass road in winter to avoid paying the stagecoach fare.

In 1880, both the Denver, South Park & Pacific Railroad and the Denver & Rio Grande Railroad commenced service to Leadville, ringing the death knell for the pass road. The road fell into disuse and was closed from 1910 until 1949, when local residents restored it to hold the first Get Your Ass Over the Pass burro race. The race is now a well-established event, held every July.

The town of Alma Junction is located at the intersection of Mosquito Pass Road and

Approaching the summit of Mosquito Pass

the road between Alma and Fairplay. It was also called London Junction and Alma Station and, although it was never incorporated, 150 people lived there in 1884. At its peak, the population reached 300. The town served as a stop for travelers to and from Leadville and Fairplay as well as a home to those who worked in the nearby London Mines. The McLaughlin stagecoach line ran between Alma and Fairplay, providing transfers at London Junction for travelers heading west across the pass.

In 1882, a spur of the London, South Park & Leadville Railroad was completed—a six-mile segment leading from London Junction, through Park City, to the London Mountain mining area. Used for hauling ore from the London Mines, the spur was abandoned two years later when the mines closed down.

The London Mines were established in the 1870s and small settlements grew up in the area to house the miners. A concentration works was constructed at London Junction in 1883 to process ore. The South London Mine, which opened in 1874, lies on the eastern slope of Mosquito Pass. It was the terminus of the London, South Park &

Leadville spur up Mosquito Gulch. Th North London Mine was high on Londo Mountain (12,280 feet). The mine had it own boardinghouses and an aerial tram, wit wooden tram towers that are still visibl among the trees. The tram was constructe to span the 3,300-foot distance between th North London Mine and its mill because conventional chute was not sufficient. Ruin of cabins and the bunkhouse can be seen a the site.

The North London and South Londo Mines merge via a tunnel beneath them tha goes through the mountain. In total, mor than one hundred miles of tunnels burrov through London Mountain in all direction and have yielded millions of dollars' wortl of ore.

Description

The route commences at Alma Junction, th intersection of Colorado 9 and Mosquit Pass Road (County 12), which was the junc tion of the railway spur to the London Mil and the main line.

The easy 2WD road continues past th town of Park City, an old stagecoach stop nd then past the Orphan Boy Mine, which perated well into the twentieth century, at ie 3.3-mile point. At the 4.4-mile point, ie route continues past the intersection of R 696 on the left, which travels around the outh of London Mountain and reconnects ith the pass road but is usually closed to irough traffic. A couple of miles further, FR 2 turns left, crosses Mosquito Creek, and ommences the ascent toward the pass, pro-iding scenic views of the valley.

The side road to Cooney Lake has several reek crossings and passes through the water t the bottom tip of the lake. The water at iese crossings can be over eighteen inches eep, and the road can be very rutted and oggy in places. It is an interesting 4WD oad but considerably more challenging than ie main pass road.

At the summit, the view is spectacular: outh Park spreads out to the east, and to the est is Leadville, Turquoise Lake, and the iassive Sawatch Range with its fifteen four-eners, including the three highest peaks in ie Rockies.

The road descending toward Leadville, though it begins steeply, is generally easier ian the road on the east side. About 1.5 iiles from the summit, a track to Birdseye iulch intersects on the right. This road eads north toward Colorado 91 but has ome extremely boggy sections at about the .5-mile point. To avoid damage to the ter-ain, do not attempt this trail without a 'inch (and a long winch extension strap to each the sometimes-distant winching oints).

The main road from this point affords a raightforward drive into Leadville, past lorace Tabor's Matchless Mine.

urrent Road Conditions

ike National Forest
eadville Ranger District
10 Front Street, Leadville, CO 80461
'19) 486-0749

lap References

'SFS Pike NF
San Isabel NF

USGS Lake County
Park County #1
Trails Illustrated, #109
The Roads of Colorado, p. 86
Colorado Atlas & Gazetteer, pp. 47–48

Route Directions

▼ 0.0   Start at Alma Junction, which is the intersection of Colorado 9 and County/FR 12, 1.3 miles south of Alma. Turn onto County 12, zero trip meter, and proceed west along Mosquito Pass Road. Sign points toward Mosquito Gulch.
7.8 ▲   End at intersection with Colorado 9.
         GPS: N 39°16.23′ W 106°02.83′

▼ 0.1   SO Site of cabins and other buildings that were part of Alma Junction. Grade of old railroad wye is visible between the river and the highway.
7.7 ▲   SO Site of cabins and other buildings that were part of Alma Junction. Grade of old railroad wye is visible between the river and the highway.

▼ 2.4   SO Road on right to Park City Cemetery.
5.4 ▲   SO Road on left to Park City Cemetery.

▼ 2.5   SO Site of Park City, a stage stop that grew into a town.
5.3 ▲   SO Site of Park City, a stage stop that grew into a town.

▼ 3.3   SO Orphan Boy Mine.
4.5 ▲   SO Orphan Boy Mine.

▼ 4.4   SO Intersection. Remain on FR 12. South London Mine ruins are to the left along FR 696.
3.4 ▲   SO Intersection. Remain on FR 12. South London Mine ruins are to the right along FR 696.
         GPS: N 39°16.72′ W 106°07.29′

▼ 5.4   SO View of wooden tram towers in trees on slope to the left.
2.4 ▲   SO View of wooden tram towers in trees on slope to the right.

▼ 6.2   SO Track on left to North London Mill and tailings dump.

1.6 ▲   SO Track on right to North London Mill and tailings dump.

▼ 6.7   TL Intersection. Turn left, remaining on FR 12. On the right is FR 856. Then cross creek.

1.1 ▲   TR Cross creek. Intersection. On the left is FR 856.

▼ 6.8   SO Mosquito Pass sign and Mosquito Pass Historic Stage Route marker.

1.0 ▲   SO Mosquito Pass Historic Stage Route marker.
        GPS: N 39°17.97′ W 106°09.28′

▼ 7.4   SO Track on right to Champaign Mine.

0.4 ▲   SO Track on left to Champaign Mine.

▼ 7.5   SO Cross through creek.

0.3 ▲   SO Cross through creek.

▼ 7.8   TL Intersection. Road on right goes to Cooney Lake. Zero trip meter.

0.0 ▲   Continue along FR 12.
        GPS: N 39°17.46′ W 106°09.67′

▼ 0.0   Continue along FR 12.

1.7 ▲   BR Intersection. Side road to Cooney Lake. Zero trip meter.

▼ 0.1   SO North London Mine on left.

1.6 ▲   SO North London Mine on right.

▼ 0.2   SO Track on right and mining machinery on left.

1.5 ▲   SO Mining machinery on right and track on left.

▼ 0.7   SO Track on left (FR 696) is gated farther on.

1.0 ▲   SO Track on right dead-ends.

▼ 1.7   SO Tracks on the left and right. Then summit of Mosquito Pass. Zero trip meter.

0.0 ▲   Proceed toward Leadville. Mosquito Pass Road changes to FR 12 on this side.

        GPS: N 39°16.86′ W 106°11.12′

▼ 0.0   Proceed toward Leadville. Mosquito Pass Road changes to FR 438 on this side.

7.2 ▲   SO Summit of Mosquito Pass. Tracks on the left and right. Zero trip meter.

▼ 0.3   BL Bypass trail on right is one-way downhill and rejoins at 0.8 miles.

6.9 ▲   SO Track from 6.4-mile point rejoins on left.

▼ 0.4   SO Track on left.

6.8 ▲   SO Track on right.

▼ 0.8   SO Track from 0.3-mile point rejoins on right.

6.4 ▲   BR Track on left (no entry—one way).

▼ 1.4   SO Track to Birdseye Gulch on right. Stay on main road toward Leadville.

5.8 ▲   SO Track on left to Birdseye Gulch. Stay on main road toward Mosquito Pass.
        GPS: N 39°16.15′ W 106°11.74′

▼ 2.8   TL Road forks. Stay to the left.

4.4 ▲   BR Road forks. Stay to the right.
        GPS: N 39°15.69′ W 106°13.15′

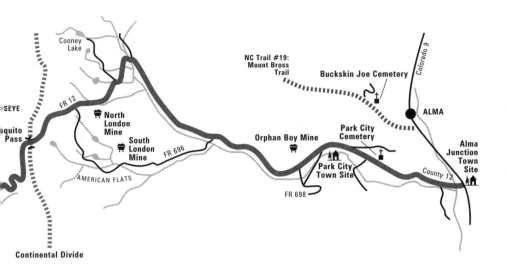

▼ 3.0	SO	Cross over creek. Then gate to Diamond Mine on left. Follow main road.		
.2 ▲	SO	Gate to Diamond Mine on right. Cross over creek.		
		GPS: N 39°15.57′ W 106°13.06′		

▼ 3.2	TR	Intersection.
.0 ▲	TL	Intersection.

▼ 3.3	SO	Mine structure on right.
.9 ▲	SO	Mine structure on left.

▼ 3.6	SO	Cross over creek.
.6 ▲	SO	Cross over creek.

▼ 3.8	SO	Mine on right and left.
.4 ▲	SO	Mine on right and left.

▼ 4.6	SO	Road on left.
.6 ▲	SO	Road on right.

▼ 5.4	SO	Intersection. Road on right.
.8 ▲	SO	Intersection. Road on left.

5.6	SO	Road on left.
.6 ▲	SO	Road on right.

▼ 6.0	SO	Matchless Mine on right.

1.2 ▲	SO	Matchless Mine on left.

▼ 6.9	SO	Leadville, Colorado & Southern Railway station on right.
0.3 ▲	SO	Leadville, Colorado & Southern Railway station on left.

▼ 7.2		End at intersection of 7th Street and Harrison Avenue in Leadville.
0.0 ▲		At the intersection of Harrison Avenue and 7th Street in Leadville, zero trip meter and proceed east along 7th Street.
		GPS: N 39°14.99′ W 106°17.47′

Mount Bross Trail

STARTING POINT Alma
FINISHING POINT Summit of Mount Bross
TOTAL MILEAGE 10.4 miles
UNPAVED MILEAGE 10.4 miles
DRIVING TIME 1 1/2 hours (one-way)
ROUTE ELEVATION 10,400 feet to 14,172 feet
USUALLY OPEN Late June to late September
DIFFICULTY RATING 5
SCENIC RATING 10

Special Attractions

- One of the highest roads in the United States.
- Stunning, panoramic views.
- Challenging shelf road.
- Numerous old mines and side trails.

History

Mount Bross has the broadest, roundest summit of any of Colorado's fifty-four fourteen-thousand-foot peaks. It was named for William Bross, a local miner and former lieutenant governor of Illinois. Bross climbed Mount Lincoln, the peak closely adjoining Mount Bross, with Father Dyer in 1876. He talked so much of the view from the summit that the local miners began calling the peak to the south Mount Bross.

Mining in the area commenced with gold strikes in the 1860s. By 1861, Quartzville, located on the northeastern slope of Mount Bross on the creek between it and Mount Lincoln, had fifty cabins. With the secon mining boom in the 1880s (this one base on silver), the town population peaked a two thousand; but the ore was not as good a hoped, and the town could not survive th silver crash of 1893.

Description

This route starts in the township of Alm. Initially, the road is graded dirt road, bu depending on how long it has been since th road has been graded, it may have some larg potholes! It passes Buckskin Joe Cemeter and town site.

After about 5.5 miles, near the Minera Park Mine, the road narrows to a 4WD roa as it starts to ascend Mount Bross and rise above timberline. Shortly after Mineral Par Mine, you'll pass Windy Ridge Bristlecon Pine Scenic Area. Information about thes ancient trees can be found on the boards a the site.

Upon passing timberline, the road gain altitude quickly. Although the surface of th road is a bit loose, it is in good condition, an you should have no problems with traction. A you progress up the mountain, there ar numerous tracks to complicate navigation although many of the tracks rejoin the mai road farther on. At about seven miles, the roa proceeds along a shelf that drops off steeply. A this point, the road becomes narrow, makin passing difficult in some sections.

As you continue up Mount Bross, you' see remains of the Dolly Varden Mine an numerous open mine shafts. Continuing you pass a miner's cabin with one of the bes living-room views in Colorado! The roa continues right to the summit. At 14,17 feet, it is one of the highest roads in th country—higher than either the road u Pikes Peak or the end of the roadway o Mount Evans.

Note that at times near the summit, ther are so many tracks, in such close succession that it was impossible to include them all i the route directions below. Follow the mai road, which switchbacks its way right to th summit.

In its upper reaches this road is prone t

The front door of the miner's cabin with a million-dollar view

e panoramic view from a section of shelf road on Mt. Bross

ock slides and erosion. You may need to divert onto one of the alternative routes to the summit. At times erosion can also make the trail dangerously narrow and unstable. Exercise caution.

From the summit, it looks as though a road traverses the ridge to Mount Lincoln. However, it does not go through and turning around is difficult. The road that once ascended Mount Lincoln is now closed.

Current Road Conditions
Park County Tourism Office
01 Main Street, Fairplay, CO 80440
719) 836-4279

Map References
USFS   Pike NF
USGS   Park County #1
Trails Illustrated, #109
The Roads of Colorado, p. 86
Colorado Atlas & Gazetteer, p. 48

Route Directions

0.0		In Alma, at the intersection of Colorado 9 and County 8, zero trip meter and proceed west along County 8 (Buckskin Road). Cross next intersection and continue on Buckskin Road toward Kite Lake.

GPS: N 39°17.04′ W 106°03.74′

▼ 1.1	SO	Track on right.
▼ 1.4	SO	Site of Buckskin Joe mining town and track on right to Buckskin Joe Cemetery (now Alma Cemetery).
▼ 1.6	SO	Track on left to Buckskin Joe Mine.
▼ 2.6	SO	Paris Mill on left.
▼ 2.7	TR	Intersection. Make sharp turn toward Windy Ridge on County 787 (FR 415).

GPS: N 39°17.79′ W 106°06.46′

▼ 3.2	SO	Paris Mine on left.
▼ 3.3	SO	Cabin on right.
▼ 4.2	SO	Track on right to cabin and Sweet Home Mine.
▼ 5.5	SO	Mineral Park Mine.

GPS: N 39°19.03′ W 106°05.03′

▼ 5.7	BR	Fork in road. FR 857 goes to the left. Shortly after, cross through creek.
▼ 6.2	SO	Windy Ridge Bristlecone Pine Scenic Area on right.

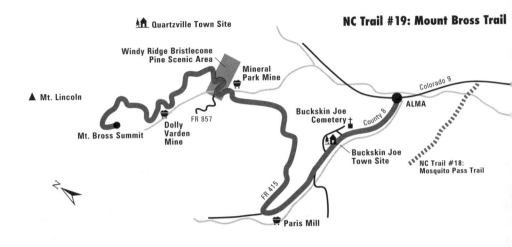

▲ Quartzville Town Site

Windy Ridge Bristlecone
Pine Scenic Area

Mineral
Park Mine

▲ Mt. Lincoln

Colorado 9

FR 857

Dolly
Varden
Mine

Mt. Bross Summit

ALMA

Buckskin Joe
Cemetery †

County 8

Buckskin Joe
Town Site

NC Trail #18:
Mosquito Pass Trail

FR 415

Paris Mill

▼ 6.4	BL	Fork in road. Mine building on right.
▼ 6.7	SO	Two tracks join on right (one closed).
▼ 7.4	BL	Fork in road. FR 415 goes to the right and is an alternative way to reach the summit. Zero trip meter.

GPS: N 39°19.53′ W 106°05.66′

▼ 0.0		Continue along track.
▼ 0.3	BR	Fork in road. Track to the Dolly Varden Mine is to the left.

GPS: N 39°19.56′ W 106°05.91′

▼ 1.3	SO	Track on right. (If you turn here, you go back down the mountain.)
▼ 1.4	SO	Cabin ruin and mine on right with a great view!
▼ 1.6	SO	Track on left and open mine portals along road on left.
▼ 1.7	SO	Track enters on right.
▼ 1.9	BL	Track enters on right.
▼ 2.0	SO	Track enters on right.
▼ 2.1	SO	Series of open mine portals on left.

GPS: N 39°20.21′ W 106°06.12′

▼ 2.2	SO	Track on left.
▼ 2.4	SO	Track on left.
▼ 2.8	BL/BR	Track on right. Then track on left.
▼ 2.8	BR	Track on left. Continue toward summit.
▼ 3.0		Mount Bross marker. 100 yards farther is the summit.

GPS: N 39°20.15′ W 106°06.42′

Hagerman Pass Trail

STARTING POINT Leadville
FINISHING POINT Basalt
TOTAL MILEAGE 62.1 miles
UNPAVED MILEAGE 21.7 miles
DRIVING TIME 3 hours
ROUTE ELEVATION 6,600 feet to 11,982 feet
USUALLY OPEN Mid-July to late September
DIFFICULTY RATING 3
SCENIC RATING 7

Special Attractions

- Historic railroad route.
- Network of 4WD trails.

History

Hagerman Pass Road is the product of one of the great railroad stories of the 1880s, the golden period of railroad expansion in Colorado. The pass was named for James J. Hagerman, the president of the Colorado Midland Railroad. Previously it had been known as Cooke Pass, and before that, the Hayden survey party had called it Frying Pan Pass in 1873.

In 1885, the Colorado Midland Railway began construction on a railway running from Aspen to Leadville. The railway was remarkable at that time because it was a standard

The famous railroad trestle bridge near Hagerman Tunnel

ard-gauge track rather than the prevalent
arrow-gauge. To enable trains to cross the
ontinental Divide, the company com-
enced construction of the Hagerman
unnel in 1885, completing the project the
ollowing year. It was 2,164 feet long and
cated only 450 feet from the pass's summit
11,528 feet, the highest standard-gauge
ilroad in the United States at the time. To
ach the tunnel, the tracks made three horse-
oe turns at a grade of 1.5 percent. One of
e turns was made with the
elp of an enormous 1,084-
ot curved trestle bridge.

On the east side of the
nnel was Douglass City, a
otorious mining camp that
oasted six saloons and a
rothel. The camp was home
the railroad construction
orkers as well as to miners.

The railroad opened in
887 but faced financial dif-
culties right from the start.
he operating costs were pro-
ibitive. Six locomotives had
operate full-time to clear

the rails in the winter, embankments collapsed from water damage, and the trestle
bridge required constant upkeep. In 1893,
the rail line was closed, and the train was
rerouted to the new Busk-Ivanhoe Tunnel
that had been constructed six hundred feet
lower. The new tunnel had proved much
more difficult to build than anticipated
because of liquid mud floods. When completed, it was nearly two miles long, 15 feet
wide, and 21 feet high. Construction had

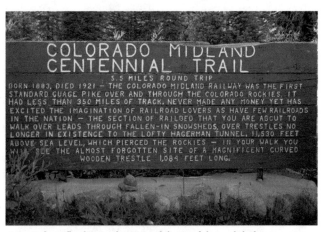

A sign at the trailhead to Douglass City and the site of the trestle bridge

taken three years, claimed twenty lives, and cost three times the budget of $1 million.

In 1897, after suffering continuous financial troubles since its formation, the Colorado Midland Railway was sold at a foreclosure. The new owners initially reverted to using the Hagerman Tunnel but went back to the Busk-Ivanhoe Tunnel in 1899. From 1922 until 1943, after the tracks had been torn up, the Busk-Ivanhoe Tunnel was known as the Carlton Tunnel and used as State Highway 104. As it was only wide enough for a single lane of motor vehicles, an alternating system of traffic control was used. A water pipeline laid through the tunnel to transfer water from the western slope of the Rockies to the east is still in use today.

In the 1960s, a new tunnel was built to divert additional water to the eastern slope as part of the multimillion-dollar Fryingpan-Arkansas Project, which provides electricity to many Front Range cities. This lower four-mile-long tunnel is known as the Charles H. Bousted Tunnel.

Description

The Hagerman Pass turnoff is 2.2 miles past the Turquoise Lake dam wall. The road is not difficult, but high clearance is recommended. In the narrower sections, adequate pull-offs facilitate passing. Below timberline, the road travels through pine and aspen forest.

The east entrance to the Carlton (Busk-Ivanhoe) Tunnel is about 3.5 miles along Hagerman Pass Road. A mile farther on is a hiking trail that leads to the remains of Douglass City, the site of the trestle bridge, Hagerman Lake, and the east entrance of the Hagerman Tunnel. It is an easy walk along the old railway grade that takes about two hours and thirty minutes.

The road continues through the pine forest that opens before the summit to an impressive view. Also evident is the high-voltage line between Denver and Grand Junction; the Hagerman Pass Road was used in the construction of the line.

On the west side of the pass, a turnoff provides an opportunity to visit Ivanhoe Lake and the west side of the Carlton (Busk-Ivanhoe) Tunnel. Hell Gate gauging station is ahead on the left, a scenic stop on the Colorado Midland Railroad.

The road, which continues past the open expanse of Sellar Park, becomes an easy 2WD road before returning to pavement about fourteen miles from the summit.

Current Road Conditions

San Isabel National Forest
Leadville Ranger District
810 Front Street, Leadville, CO 80461
(719) 486-0749

Map References

USFS   San Isabel NF
       White River NF
USGS   Lake County
       Pitkin County #2
       Eagle County #3
Trails Illustrated, #109, #110, #126, #127
The Roads of Colorado, pp. 68–69, 85–86
Colorado Atlas & Gazetteer, pp. 46–47

Route Directions

▼ 0.0   In Leadville, from the intersection of West 6th Street and Harrison Avenue zero trip meter and proceed west from the traffic light toward Turquoise Lake
7.5 ▲   End at intersection with Harrison Avenue in Leadville.
         GPS: N 39°14.93' W 106°17.49'

▼ 0.8   TR Stop sign.
6.7 ▲   TL Stop sign.

▼ 3.0   SO Cross railway line.
4.5 ▲   SO Cross railway line.

▼ 3.4   BR Fork in road.
4.1 ▲   BL Road on right.

▼ 4.1   SO Road on right.
3.4 ▲   SO Road on left.

▼ 4.3   SO Dam wall-Turquoise Lake.
3.2 ▲   SO Dam wall-Turquoise Lake.

▼ 5.6   SO Road on right.

C Trail #20: Hagerman Pass Trail

.9 ▲	SO	Road on left.
▼ 7.5	BL	Onto Hagerman Pass Road (FR 105). Zero trip meter.
▮.0 ▲		Proceed along Turquoise Lake Road. **GPS: N 39°16.12' W 106°25.00'**
▼ 0.0		Proceed along FR 105.
▮.6 ▲	TR	Onto Turquoise Lake Road. Zero trip meter.
▼ 1.7	SO	Track on left is Sugarloaf Mountain Road (FR 105.1A).
▮.9 ▲	SO	Track on right is Sugarloaf Mountain Road (FR 105.1A).
▼ 3.4	SO	Cross over Busk Creek.
▮.2 ▲	SO	Cross over Busk Creek.
▼ 3.5	BR	East entrance (sealed) of the Carlton (Busk-Ivanhoe) Tunnel on left.
▮.1 ▲	BL	East entrance (sealed) of the Carlton (Busk-Ivanhoe) Tunnel on right.
▼ 4.5	SO	Colorado Midland Centennial Trail marker on left. Walking trail to trestle, tunnel, and Hagerman Lake via TR 1491.
▮.1 ▲	SO	Colorado Midland Centennial Trail marker on right. Walking trail to trestle, tunnel, and Hagerman Lake via TR 1491. **GPS: N 39°15.56' W 106°27.51'**
▼ 6.4	SO	Track on right to Skinner Hut.

1.2 ▲	SO	Track on left to Skinner Hut.
▼ 7.1	SO	Seasonal closure gate.
0.5 ▲	SO	Seasonal closure gate.
▼ 7.6	SO	Hagerman Pass summit. Zero trip meter.
0.0 ▲		Continue along FR 105.
▼ 0.0		Continue along FR 105. **GPS: N 39°15.80' W 106°28.83'**
14.0 ▲	SO	Hagerman Pass summit. Zero trip meter.
▼ 3.6	SO	Seasonal gate.
10.4 ▲	SO	Seasonal gate.
▼ 3.7	SO	Intersection with FR 532 on the right and FR 527 (to Ivanhoe Lake) on the left. Remain on FR 105 and follow sign to Ruedi Reservoir.
10.3 ▲	SO	Remain on 105 and follow sign to Hagerman Pass.
▼ 4.9	SO	Track on right.
9.1 ▲	SO	Track on left.
▼ 5.3	SO	Hell Gate scenic overlook and gauging station in the valley on left among trees.
8.7 ▲	SO	Hell Gate scenic overlook and gauging station in the valley on right among trees.
▼ 10.9	SO	Sellar Park on left. Track on right goes

to Diemer Lake and up to North Fork Road.

▲ 3.1 SO Sellar Park on right. Track on left goes to Diemer Lake and up to North Fork Road.
GPS: N 39°19.21′ W 106°36.63′

▼ 14.0 BR Intersection with road on left. Proceed onto paved Fryingpan Road. Zero trip meter.

0.0 ▲ Continue along main road.
GPS: N 39°17.89′ W 106°35.21′

▼ 0.0 Continue along main road.
33.0 ▲ BL Intersection. Continue toward Hagerman Pass on unpaved FR 105. Zero trip meter.

▼ 0.1 SO Road on left to Fryingpan Lakes Trailhead.
32.9 ▲ SO Road on right to Fryingpan Lakes Trailhead.

▼ 3.4 SO USFS Chapman Dam Campground.
29.6 ▲ SO USFS Chapman Dam Campground.

▼ 3.7 SO USFS Chapman Dam Campground.
29.3 ▲ SO USFS Chapman Dam Campground.

▼ 6.9 SO Road on right is North-Central #21: Brush Creek to Crooked Creek Pass Trail. It goes to Eagle.
26.1 ▲ SO Road on left is North-Central #21: Brush Creek to Crooked Creek Pass Trail. It goes to Eagle.
GPS: N 39°21.10′ W 106°41.30′

▼ 8.2 SO Thomasville.
24.8 ▲ SO Thomasville.

▼ 9.6 SO Meredith.
23.6 ▲ SO Meredith.

▼ 10.0 SO Ruedi Reservoir on left.
23.0 ▲ SO Ruedi Reservoir on right.

▼ 30.7 SO Basalt.
2.3 ▲ SO Leaving Basalt.

▼ 30.9 TR Intersection with Midland and Two Rivers Road (Business Route 82).
2.1 ▲ TL Intersection with Fryingpan Road.

▼ 33.0 End at intersection with 82 in Basalt.
0.0 ▲ From traffic light at intersection of Colorado 82 and Business Route 82 (Two Rivers Road), zero trip meter and proceed along Business Route 82 toward Basalt.
GPS: N 39°22.27′ W 107°04.23′

Brush Creek to Crooked Creek Pass Trail

STARTING POINT Eagle
FINISHING POINT Intersection of North-Central #20: Hagerman Pass Trail (County 104) and FR 400, 0.5 miles east of Thomasville
TOTAL MILEAGE 30.8 miles
UNPAVED MILEAGE 20.6 miles
DRIVING TIME 1 1/2 hours
ROUTE ELEVATION 6,600 feet to 9,995 feet
USUALLY OPEN Early June to early November
DIFFICULTY RATING 2
SCENIC RATING 7

Special Attractions

- Varied forest scenery along an easy 4WD trail.
- Access to a network of 4WD trails.

Description

This route starts in Eagle and follows the Brush Creek Valley through attractive ranch land; it is paved for the first ten miles before the road forks. The route follows the right-hand fork toward Sylvan Lake.

After Sylvan Lake the road narrows but remains an easy 2WD road to Crooked Creek Pass. Although there are sections of shelf road with high drop-offs from the edge of the road, the road remains relatively wide and does not rank as a scary Colorado shelf road.

From the gentle pass, the road descends

hrough similar countryside, traveling hrough Crooked Creek Park and then eside Crooked Creek Reservoir, taking several sharp bends before reaching Fryingpan Road approximately half a mile east of the own site of Thomasville, an old railroad tation along the Colorado Midland Railway line.

urrent Road Conditions

White River National Forest
Eagle Ranger District
25 West 5th Street, Eagle, CO 81631
970) 328-6388

Map References

USFS White River NF
USGS Eagle County #1
      Eagle County #3
      Pitkin County #2
Trails Illustrated, #121, #126
The Roads of Colorado, p. 69
Colorado Atlas & Gazetteer, pp. 36, 46–47

Route Directions

▼ 0.0   At the intersection of Grand Avenue and Broadway in Eagle, zero trip meter and proceed south along Broadway toward Sylvan Lake.

▲ 0.2   End at intersection of Grand Avenue and Broadway in Eagle.
      GPS: N 39°39.35′ W 106°49.65′

▼ 0.2   TL   Stop sign. Turn onto 5th.
▲ 10.0   TR   Onto Broadway.

▼ 0.3   TR   Onto Capitol (will become Brush Creek Road and County 307).
▲ 9.9   TL   Onto 5th.

▼ 4.1   SO   Cross over bridge.
▲ 6.1   SO   Cross over bridge.

▼ 6.1   SO   Cross over bridge.
▲ 4.1   SO   Cross over bridge.

▼ 9.5   SO   Enter White River National Forest. Road becomes FR 400.
▲ 0.7   SO   Leave White River National Forest.

NC Trail #21: Brush Creek to Crooked Creek Pass Trail

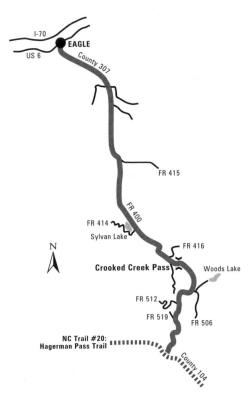

Road becomes County 307.

▼ 10.2   BR   Road forks. Left goes to Yeoman Park and Fulford.
▲ 0.0   Continue on FR 400.
      GPS: N 39°32.35′ W 106°45.14′

▼ 0.0   Proceed along FR 400 toward Sylvan Lake and Fryingpan River.
▲ 9.7   BL   Intersection.

▼ 1.2   SO   Cross over creek.
▲ 8.4   SO   Cross over creek.

▼ 2.3   SO   Walking trail on right to McKenzie Gulch.
▲ 7.4   SO   Walking trail on left to McKenzie Gulch.

▼ 4.5   SO   Sylvan Lake entrance.
▲ 5.2   SO   Sylvan Lake entrance.

▼ 5.5   SO   FR 414 on right to Gypsum Creek and reservoir. Then seasonal gate.

4.2 ▲   SO   Seasonal gate. Track on right to Gypsum Creek and reservoir.
GPS: N 39°28.28' W 106°43.64'

▼ 7.2   SO   Track on right to FR 431.

2.4 ▲   SO   Track on left to FR 431.

▼ 9.6   SO   Track on right to Red Table Mountain.

0.1 ▲   SO   Track on left to Red Table Mountain.

▼ 9.7   SO   Track on left. Cattle guard. Crooked Creek Pass. Zero trip meter.

0.0 ▲   Continue on FR 400 toward Eagle.
GPS: N 39°26.49' W 106°41.08'

▼ 0.0   Continue on FR 400.

10.9 ▲   SO   Crooked Creek Pass. Cattle guard. Track on left. Zero trip meter.

▼ 0.7   SO   Cross over creek.

10.2 ▲   SO   Cross over creek.

▼ 2.0   SO   Cross over creek.

8.8 ▲   SO   Cross over creek.

▼ 2.3   SO   Crooked Creek Reservoir on left.

8.6 ▲   SO   Crooked Creek Reservoir on right.

▼ 3.1   SO   FR 506 on left to Woods Lake. Cross over creek.

7.8 ▲   SO   Cross over creek. FR 506 on left to Woods Lake.

▼ 5.0   SO   FR 512 on right.

5.9 ▲   SO   FR 512 on left.
GPS: N 39°24.18' W 106°40.53'

▼ 7.0   SO   FR 519 on right. Then cattle guard.

3.8 ▲   SO   Cattle guard. FR 519 on right.

▼ 8.3   SO   Seasonal gate.

2.5 ▲   SO   Seasonal gate.

▼ 8.5   SO   Cross over creek.

2.3 ▲   SO   Cross over creek.

▼ 0.1   SO   Bridge over creek.

0.8 ▲   SO   Bridge over creek.

▼ 10.9   End at intersection with Fryingpan Road, about 0.5 miles east of Thomasville. This is the western portion of North-Central #20: Hagerman Pass Trail.

0.0 ▲   At intersection of North-Central #20: Hagerman Pass Trail (Fryingpan Road/County 104) and FR 400, zero trip meter and proceed north on FR 400. This intersection is about 0.5 miles east of Thomasville.
GPS: N 39°21.10' W 106°41.30'

Cottonwood Pass Trail

STARTING POINT   Gypsum
FINISHING POINT   Intersection of Colorado 82 and Garfield County 113
TOTAL MILEAGE   26.5 miles
UNPAVED MILEAGE   16.1 miles
DRIVING TIME   1 1/4 hours
ROUTE ELEVATION   6,100 feet to 8,280 feet
USUALLY OPEN   Early July to early November
DIFFICULTY RATING   2
SCENIC RATING   7

Special Attractions

- Easy, scenic, historic 4WD trail.
- Access to a network of 4WD trails.

History

Cottonwood Pass Trail is about sixty miles northwest of the other, better-known Cottonwood Pass that links Buena Vista with Taylor Park. In use from 1873, this pass was upgraded to a wagon road in 1883 to provide access from Gypsum into the north end of the booming Roaring Fork Valley. Until World War II, Cottonwood Pass was one of the major pass routes in Colorado and was a primary route between Denver and Grand Junction. Later, a major highway route was constructed through Glenwood Canyon.

Trail #22: Cottonwood Pass Trail

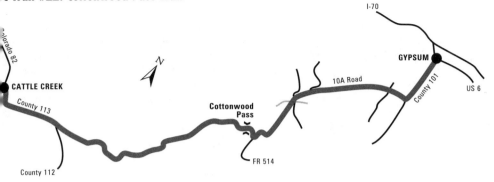

Description

From Gypsum to the pass, the road travels through land owned by the Bureau of Land Management, and used for ranching. It passes through gentle, rolling hills and a broad valley before climbing through the corner of the White River National Forest.

From the pass, the road descends through similar country but provides views of several Elk Range fourteeners, including Snowmass Mountain and Mount Sopris. The road continues beside Cattle Creek before exiting on Colorado 82.

In dry conditions, the road is relatively easy—even for 2WD vehicles—but it can become impassable after rain, especially on the north side of the pass.

Current Road Conditions

White River National Forest
Eagle Ranger District
125 West 5th Street, Eagle, CO 81631
(970) 328-6388

Map References

USFS   White River NF
USGS   Eagle County #3
        Garfield County #5
The Roads of Colorado, pp. 68–69
Colorado Atlas & Gazetteer, pp. 36, 45–46

Route Directions

▼ 0.0   At intersection of Valley Road and US 6 in Gypsum, zero trip meter and pro-

ceed south along Valley Road.

11.1 ▲   End at T-intersection with US 6 in Gypsum.
           GPS: N 39°38.69′ W 106°56.90′

▼ 1.9   TR   Follow Cottonwood Pass sign.
9.2 ▲   TL   T-intersection with Valley Road (County 101).
             GPS: N 39°36.99′ W 106°56.90′

▼ 2.7   SO   Cross bridge.
8.4 ▲   SO   Cross bridge.

▼ 3.3   TR   Follow Cottonwood Pass sign.
7.8 ▲   TL   T-intersection and stop sign.
             GPS: N 39°36.53′ W 106°58.04′

▼ 3.5   SO   Cattle guard.
7.6 ▲   SO   Cattle guard. Pavement.

▼ 4.1   SO   Road on right. Cattle guard.
7.0 ▲   SO   Cattle guard. Road on left.

▼ 4.8   SO   Track on left.
6.2 ▲   SO   Track on right.

▼ 6.4   SO   Track on left.
4.6 ▲   SO   Track on right.

▼ 7.4   SO   Track on right.
3.7 ▲   SO   Track on left.

▼ 8.2   SO   Track on right.
2.9 ▲   SO   Track on left.

▼ 8.3	SO	Track on left. Cross over creek.
2.8 ▲	SO	Cross over creek. Track on right.

▼ 11.1	SO	Red Table Road (FR 514) on left. Zero trip meter.
0.0 ▲		Continue along 10A.
		GPS: N 39°31.80′ W 107°02.78′

▼ 0.0		Continue along main road.
15.4 ▲	SO	Red Table Road (FR 514) on right. Zero trip meter.

▼ 0.8	SO	Cottonwood Pass (unmarked).
14.5 ▲	SO	Cottonwood Pass (unmarked).
		GPS: N 39°31.83′ W 107°03.49′

▼ 5.5	SO	Enter Garfield County. Name of road changes to County 113.
9.8 ▲	SO	Road becomes County 10A. Enter Eagle County.

▼ 7.0	BR	Stay on County 113.
8.4 ▲	BL	Intersection. Stay on 113 toward Cottonwood Pass.

▼ 7.7	BL	Stay on County 113.
7.6 ▲	BR	Fork in road. Follow County 113 toward Gypsum.

▼ 8.1	SO	Cross over creek.
7.3 ▲	SO	Cross over creek.

▼ 8.5	BR	Road on left. Pavement.
6.9 ▲	BL	Onto unpaved road. Road on right.

▼ 12.1	SO	County 112 on the left.
3.3 ▲	SO	County 112 on the right.

▼ 15.4		End at intersection with County 82 in Cattle Creek.
0.0 ▲		Begin in Cattle Creek, between Glenwood Springs and Carbondale on County 82. Zero trip meter at the intersection of County 82 and Cattle Creek Road (County 113) and proceed east along the paved road.
		GPS: N 39°27.48′ W 107°15.68′

Crooked Creek Trail

STARTING POINT Intersection of FR 138 and Crooked Creek Road (FR 139)
FINISHING POINT Fraser
TOTAL MILEAGE 18.5 miles
UNPAVED MILEAGE 16.7 miles
DRIVING TIME 1 hour
ROUTE ELEVATION 8,400 feet to 9,800 feet
USUALLY OPEN May to early December
DIFFICULTY RATING 1
SCENIC RATING 7

Special Attractions

- Easy, 4WD trail through Arapaho National Forest.
- Backbone of an extensive network of 4WD trails.
- Good backcountry camping.

Description

Access to this trail can be either north from I-70 at Silverthorne or south from Parshall on US 40. From I-70 at Silverthorne, you travel about 12.5 miles north on Colorado 9 to Ute Pass Road. Turn right onto Ute Pass Road (FR132) and follow this for 8 miles then bear left when FR 138 enters from the right. Go another 3.5 miles and turn right onto FR 139. From Parshall, just east of town turn right onto County 3 following a sign to Williams Fork Reservoir. About 15 miles farther, FR 139 is on the left at the USFS Horseshoe Campground.

This trail is the backbone for numerous trails in the area. In dry conditions, most are only moderately difficult. There are numerous good backcountry camping spots that are well utilized in hunting season.

FR 139 is an easy, maintained road that is suitable for cars in dry conditions. It travels through spruce and pine forest initially beside Keyser Creek. The forest is interspersed with attractive rocky outcrops and occasional views of nearby mountain ranges.

Three or four miles before Fraser, near the

▲ section of trail typical of this route

end of the trail, there is considerable road-
work. The key is to remain on the main road.

Current Road Conditions
Arapaho and Roosevelt National Forest
Sulphur Ranger District
9 Ten Mile Drive, Granby, CO 80446
(970) 887-4100

Map References
USFS Arapaho & Roosevelt NF
USGS Grand County #3
       Grand County #4
Trails Illustrated, #103, #107
The Roads of Colorado, pp. 70–71
Colorado Atlas & Gazetteer, pp. 38–39

Route Directions

▼ 0.0   From the intersection of FR 138 and FR
         139, zero trip meter and proceed east
         along FR 139.
6.4 ▲   End at intersection with (FR 138).
         N39°54.00' W106°05.79'

▼ 0.1   SO USFS Horseshoe Campground on left,
             then bridge over Williams Fork.
6.3 ▲   SO Bridge over Williams Fork, then
             Horseshoe Campground on right.

▼ 0.8   SO Keyser Ridge Road on right leads to
             Keyser Ridge hiking trail (TR 140).
5.6 ▲   SO Track on left is Keyser Ridge Road,
             leading to Keyser Ridge hiking trail.
             N39°53.75' W106°04.94'

▼ 3.0   SO Cook Creek Road (FR 253) on left.
3.4 ▲   TR Cook Creek Road (FR 253) on right.
             N39°54.42' W106°02.70'

▼ 4.6   TL Intersection. Remain on FR 139.
             Straight ahead is FR 136 to Lake
             Evelyn Trailhead and Bottle Pass Trail.
1.8 ▲   BR Toward Parshall on FR 139.
             N39°54.46' W106°01.00'

▼ 6.5   BR North-Central #25: Muddy Creek Trail
             (FR 134) on left. Zero trip meter.

NC Trail #23: Crooked Creek Trail

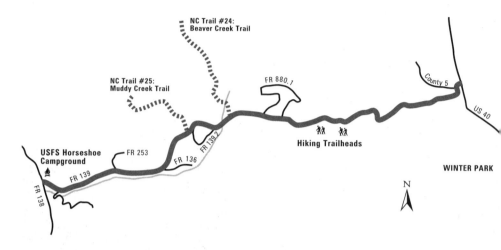

0.0 ▲   Continue along FR 139.
N39°55.68′ W106°00.21′

▼ 0.0   Continue along main trail.
1.9 ▲   BL   North-Central #25: Muddy Creek Trail (FR 134) on right. Zero trip meter.

▼ 0.1   BL   FR 139.2 on right.
1.7 ▲   BR   FR 139.2 on left.

▼ 0.8   SO   139.2 on right.
1.0 ▲   SO   FR 139.2 on left.

▼ 1.5   BL   Cross over creek, then FR 879 on right.
0.4 ▲   SO   FR 879 on left, then cross over creek.

▼ 1.9   BR   North-Central #24: Beaver Creek Trail (FR 133) on left, which goes through to US 40. Zero trip meter.
0.0 ▲   SO   Continue on main road toward Horseshoe Campground.
N 39°56.18′ W 105°58.45′

▼ 0.0   SO   Continue along FR 139.
10.1 ▲   BL   North-Central #24: Beaver Creek Trail (FR 133) on right. Zero trip meter.

▼ 0.6   SO   FR 880.2 on left.
9.5 ▲   SO   FR 880.2 on right.

▼ 1.1   SO   Track on left is FR 880.1 to Rocky Point.

9.0 ▲   SO   Track on right is also FR 880.1 to Rocky Point.
N 39°56.30′ W 105°57.20′

▼ 1.7   SO   Track on left is also FR 880.1 to Rocky Point.
8.4 ▲   SO   Track on right is FR 880.1 to Rocky Point.
N 39°56.22′ W 105°56.58′

▼ 1.9   SO   FR 882.1 on right.
8.2 ▲   SO   FR 882.1 on left.

▼ 3.4   SO   Cattle guard.
6.7 ▲   SO   Cattle guard.

▼ 3.7   SO   Tracks on right. One is portion of Backscratch and Tipperary Creek Trailheads.
6.4 ▲   SO   Two tracks on left. One is portion of Backscratch and Tipperary Creek Trailheads.

▼ 4.7   SO   Tipperary Creek Trailhead loop on right.
5.4 ▲   SO   Tipperary Creek Trailhead loop on left.

▼ 4.8   SO   Leave Arapaho National Forest. Cross cattle guard.
5.2 ▲   SO   Cattle guard. Enter Arapaho National Forest.

▼ 5.8   SO   Road on left.

.3 ▲	SO	Road on right.

▼ 6.5	SO	Road on left.
.6 ▲	SO	Road on right.

▼ 7.2	SO	County 5001 on left.
.9 ▲	TL	County 5001 on right.

▼ 8.3	SO	County 501 on right.
.8 ▲	SO	County 501 on left.

▼ 9.9	TR	Intersection with County 5.
▮.2 ▲	TL	Onto County 50 (Crooked Creek Road). County 5 goes straight on.

▼ 10.1		Cross railroad tracks and end at intersection with US 40.
▮.0 ▲		In Fraser, at the intersection of US 40 and County 5, zero trip meter and proceed west along County 5 and cross railroad tracks. This intersection is 3/4 mile north of the Fraser Visitor Center.
		N 39°57.31′ W 105°49.18′

Beaver Creek Trail

STARTING POINT Intersection of US 40 and County 50 (FR 133) between Hot Sulphur Springs and Parshall

FINISHING POINT North-Central #23: Crooked Creek Trail (FR 139)

TOTAL MILEAGE 13.9 miles

UNPAVED MILEAGE 13.9 miles

DRIVING TIME 45 minutes

ROUTE ELEVATION 7,600 feet to 10,400 feet

USUALLY OPEN Late May to late November

DIFFICULTY RATING 2

SCENIC RATING 7

Special Attractions

■ Easy side road from Crooked Creek Road (FR 139) through gentle, picturesque countryside.

■ Part of an extensive network of 4WD trails.

■ Good backcountry camping.

Description

This route climbs up gently from the Colorado River, traveling along a maintained gravel road that looks down on Beaver Creek a short distance below. As you travel along above the creek, there is plenty of evidence of the industrious beavers that gave the creek its name.

After entering the forest, the road remains easy in dry conditions, although it is not maintained. In wet conditions, sections are prone to being muddy and the road is significantly more difficult.

The route continues alongside the Blue Ridge Mountains before connecting with FR 139. The meadows in the area are filled with wildflowers in the summer, and except in hunting season, the trail is lightly used.

Current Road Conditions

Arapaho and Roosevelt National Forest
Sulphur Ranger District
9 Ten Mile Drive, Granby, CO 80446
(970) 887-4100

Map References

USFS Arapaho & Roosevelt NF
USGS Grand County #3
　　　Grand County #4
Trails Illustrated, #103, #107, #106
The Roads of Colorado, p. 54
Colorado Atlas & Gazetteer, pp. 38, 28

Route Directions

▼ 0.0		From US 40 (about halfway between Hot Sulphur Springs and Parshall), zero trip meter and proceed southeast along County 50 (FR 133). This is at the bridge over the Colorado River before entering Byers Canyon.
13.9 ▲		End at intersection with US 40.
		N 40°03.21′ W 106°07.94′

▼ 0.1	SO	State wildlife area and camping on right.
13.8 ▲	SO	State wildlife area and camping on left.

▼ 2.1	SO	Track on left.
11.8 ▲	SO	Track on right.

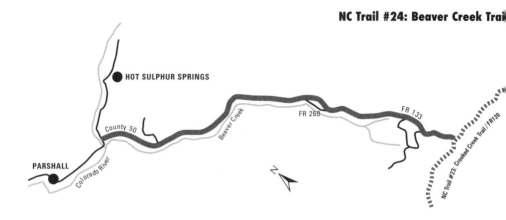

▼ 2.8	SO	Cattle guard, then enter Arapaho National Forest.
11.1 ▲	SO	Cross cattle guard.
		N 40°01.80′ W 106°06.00′

▼ 4.4	SO	Track on right with bridge and gate.
9.5 ▲	SO	Track on left.

▼ 6.1	SO	Cattle guard.
7.8 ▲	SO	Cattle guard.

▼ 7.3	SO	Track on left.
6.6 ▲	SO	Track on right.
		N 40°00.17′ W 106°02.05′

▼ 7.8	SO	FR 260 on right.
6.1 ▲	SO	FR 260 on left.

▼ 10.1	SO	Cattle guard, then FR 874 on right.
3.8 ▲	SO	FR 874 on left, then cross cattle guard.
		N 39°58.48′ W 106°00.37′

▼ 11.7	SO	FR 878 on right.
2.2 ▲	SO	FR 878 on left.

▼ 12.4	SO	Unmarked track on right.
1.5 ▲	SO	Track on left.

▼ 12.6	SO	FR 133.2 on right.
1.3 ▲	SO	FR 133.2 on left.
		N 39°56.88′ W 105°59.27′

▼ 13.9		End at intersection with North-Central #23: Crooked Creek Trail (FR 139).

0.0 ▲		From North-Central #23: Crooked Creek Trail (FR 139), zero trip meter and turn onto FR 133 (Beaver Creek Road).
		N 39°56.23′ W 105°58.47′

NORTH-CENTRAL REGION TRAIL #25

Muddy Creek Trail

STARTING POINT Intersection of Crooked Creek Road (FR 139) and FR 134

FINISHING POINT Intersection of County 3 and US 40 near Parshall

TOTAL MILEAGE 17.8 miles

UNPAVED MILEAGE 15.8 miles

DRIVING TIME 1 1/4 hours

ROUTE ELEVATION 7,600 feet to 9,900 feet

USUALLY OPEN Late May to late November

DIFFICULTY RATING 3

SCENIC RATING 8

Special Attractions

- Scenic road through Arapaho National Forest that can be used to form a loop.
- Side road to FR 139.
- The challenge of negotiating numerous mud holes.

Description

This 4WD trail is another side road to FR 139. It is a scenic road that is usually more challenging than many of the others in the

A section of the trail showing how muddy it can become, especially during hunting season

area. We have rated the trail based on dry conditions, when the greatest problem you may face is negotiating the many rutted mud holes. However, if the conditions are adverse, the trail can be impassable to stock vehicles. This is especially likely during fall hunting season when the trail is heavily used. At such times, the rating would be either 6 or 7. One fairly steep downhill section is extremely slippery when wet, which makes traveling in the southerly, or reverse, direction even more difficult. We recommend mud tires and/or chains if the weather conditions make mud likely. At times the clearance is tight as you pass between the trees, but overall the route offers little difficulty unless the road is muddy.

The route is more scenic than many in the area. There are panoramic views from the higher sections and the forest includes some sizable stands of aspen which in combination with the attractive open meadows, provide welcome variety to the scenery. As you exit the forest, the route travels through rolling range land before offering a good view of Williams Fork Reservoir.

Current Road Conditions

Arapaho and Roosevelt National Forest
Sulphur Ranger District
9 Ten Mile Drive, Granby, CO 80446
(970) 887-4100

Map References

USFS   Arapaho & Roosevelt NF
USGS   Grand County #3
          Grand County #4
Trails Illustrated, #106, #107
The Roads of Colorado, p. 54
Colorado Atlas & Gazetteer, pp. 38, 28

Route Directions

▼ 0.0   From North-Central #23: Crooked Creek Trail (FR 139), zero trip meter and turn onto Muddy Creek Road (FR 134).

10.7 ▲   End at the intersection with North-

NC Trail #25: Muddy Creek Trail

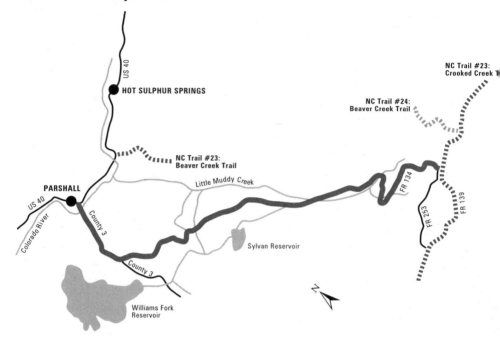

Central #23: Crooked Creek Trail
(FR 139).
N 39°55.68′ W 106°00.21′

▼ 0.1 SO Cook Creek Road (FR 253) on left.
10.6 ▲ SO Cook Creek Road (FR 253) on right.

▼ 0.8 SO Track on left.
9.9 ▲ SO Track on right.

▼ 1.0 SO Track on left.
9.7 ▲ SO Track on right.

▼ 2.9 SO Track on left.
7.8 ▲ SO Track on right.

▼ 4.5 BL Two tracks on right, then cross over
Muddy Creek.
6.1 ▲ BR Cross over Muddy Creek, then two
tracks on left.
N 39°56.87′ W 106°01.95′

▼ 5.4 SO Cross through gate (leave it as you
find it).
5.3 ▲ SO Cross through gate (leave it as you
find it).

▼ 6.1 SO Track on right.
4.6 ▲ SO Track on left.

▼ 7.0 SO Cross bridge over creek, then track on
left.
3.7 ▲ SO Track on right, then cross bridge over
creek.
N 39°57.75′ W 106°04.16′

▼ 7.0 SO Cross through gate (leave it as you
find it).
3.6 ▲ SO Cross through gate (leave it as you
find it).

▼ 7.4 SO Track on right.
3.3 ▲ SO Track on left.

▼ 7.6 SO Track on left.
3.0 ▲ SO Track on right.

▼ 7.8-8.0 SO A potentially VERY boggy section.
2.6-2.8 ▲SO A potentially VERY boggy section.

▼ 8.2 SO Tracks on left and right, then cross
over creek.

▲.4 ▲	SO	Cross over creek, then tracks on left and right.
▼ 9.5	SO	Track on right.
.1 ▲	SO	Track on left.
		N 39°59.17' W 106°05.76'
▼ 9.9	SO	Track on right.
▮.8 ▲	SO	Track on left.
▼ 10.2	SO	Track on left.
▮.4 ▲	BL	Track on right.
▼ 10.7	SO	Leave Arapaho National Forest and cross cattle guard. Name of road changes to County 340. Zero trip meter.
▮.0 ▲		Continue along route.
		N 39°59.66' W 106°06.69'
▼ 0.0		Continue along route.
▮.1 ▲	SO	Cross cattle guard and enter Arapaho National Forest. Name of road changes to FR 134. Zero trip meter.
▼ 0.5	SO	Cattle guard.
▮.6 ▲	SO	Cattle guard.
▼ 0.8	SO	Cattle guard.
▮.3 ▲	SO	Cattle guard.
▼ 2.0	SO	Cattle guard.
▮.1 ▲	SO	Cattle guard.
▼ 3.1	SO	Cattle guard.
▮.0 ▲	SO	Cattle guard.
▼ 5.1	TR	Intersection with County 3.
2.0 ▲	BL	Onto Grand County 340.
		N 40°01.76' W 106°10.86'
▼ 6.8	BR	Cross creek.
▮.3 ▲	BL	Cross creek.
▼ 7.1		End at intersection with US 40.
▮.0 ▲		At the intersection of US 40 and County 3 near Parshall, zero trip meter and proceed along County 3.
		N 40°03.10' W 106°09.91'

Yankee Hill Trail

STARTING POINT Intersection of Fall River Road (County 275) and York Gulch Road (FR 277.3)
FINISHING POINT Silver Lake
TOTAL MILEAGE 8.8 miles
UNPAVED MILEAGE 8.8 miles
DRIVING TIME 1 hour
ROUTE ELEVATION 8,100 feet to 11,000 feet
USUALLY OPEN June to October
DIFFICULTY RATING 5
SCENIC RATING 7

Special Attractions

■ Historic mining district.
■ Access to a network of 4WD trails.

History

This area was the site of the first silver discovery in Colorado in 1860, three years before the rush to the Georgetown area. However, the miners were looking for gold and had little knowledge of silver mining. That most of the mines yielded much less than had been hoped for didn't stop thousands of prospectors from pouring into the district. Ore that was mined proved expensive to mill because techniques for extracting silver were still very inefficient. The period of rapid improvement in the technology for milling and smelting silver was still a couple of years away.

The town of Fall River was soon established at the confluence of the Fall River and Clear Creek. This junction is noteworthy because it is the only location in the United States where a river flows into a creek. The town stretched along Fall River and grew to include a post office, a hotel, numerous stores, and two mills. It survived the disappointing mining results because it was located on the stage route that ran from Central City to Georgetown, across Yankee Hill. Nothing remains of Fall River; and since the 1960s, the main part of town has been buried beneath the interstate highway.

The toll gate at Fall River about 1870

Yankee was located on the south side of Yankee Hill, just below timberline. Virtually nothing remains of the town because the forest has grown over the site. The town was the junction between two stage lines that serviced the route between Central City and Georgetown. It developed as a mining camp after the discovery of rich surface gold deposits in the early 1890s. The North Star and the Gold Anchor were the largest mines. Despite the harsh winters at the elevation of nearly 11,000, the town survived into the twentieth century. It had a post office from 1893 to 1910, electricity from 1902, tele-

Ninety-Four on Yankee Hill in the early 1900s

phone service from 1903, and a mill built b the Gold Anchor in 1905.

Ninety-Four, located on the eastern slop and near the base of Yankee Hill, was name for the year it was founded: 1894. It wa merely a cluster of cabins that grew from th need to house the workers at the mines i the vicinity—the Ninety-Four, the Lalla, an the Princess Alice. Proximity to the townshi of Alice restricted its need to expansion Some structures and numerous grave mark ers remain.

Silver City, located at the headwaters o the Fall River near Silver Lake was founde in the rush of 1860. The initial enthusiasn drew up to one thousand prospectors to th area. Little silver was found and high trans portation cost made further efforts un ecomonic. The town was short-lived, lastin only a year or two, and no buildings from the era remain.

Description

To get to the beginning of this 4WD trail take exit 238 from I-70 and proceed along Fall River Road (County 275). This area wa the location of Fall River township.

About one mile along Fall River Road i the turnoff onto York Gulch Road (FR 277.3). The road starts its ascent from the river immediately, initially passing through a residential area.

At the top of the hill, the road intersects with FR 175.1. Navigation from this point is made difficult by the numerous side roads many have forest service designations to the first decimal place. Frequently, these roads are not marked on the maps of the area. There are also many private access roads, which are usually identifiable.

The road surface gets progressively more rough. The main obstacles are sections with boulders large enough to cause clearance problems and a moderately steep grade with a loose, wheel-rutted surface. Neither condition is troublesome for a 4WD vehicle in dry conditions, but together they give the road its difficulty rating of 5. In wet conditions, sections become very boggy.

The trail offers scenery that ranges from

A section of trail typical of this route

dry, gravelly country with stunted forestation to broader sweeping views, particularly on the approach to St. Mary's Glacier. Evidence of mining activity is interspersed throughout the route.

Current Road Conditions

Arapaho and Roosevelt National Forest
Clear Creek Ranger District
101 Chicago Creek
Idaho Springs, CO 80452
(303) 567-3000

Map References

USFS   Arapaho and Roosevelt NF
USGS Clear Creek County
          Gilpin County
Trails Illustrated, #103
The Roads of Colorado, p. 71
Colorado Atlas & Gazetteer, p. 39

Route Directions

▼ 0.0   At the intersection of Fall River Road (County 275) and York Gulch Road (FR 277.3), zero trip meter and proceed uphill on York Gulch Road through the residential area.

2.7 ▲   End at intersection with Fall River Road.
          N 39°46.23′ W 105°33.55′

▼ 2.7   SO Intersection. North-Central #27: Nevadaville Loop on right to Central City. To the left is FR 273.1. Zero trip meter.

0.0 ▲   Continue straight ahead on FR 277.3 and follow York Gulch sign.
          N 39°48.03′ W 105°34.16′

▼ 0.0   Continue along FR 175.1 and cross intersection with FR 401.1 on the right and closed track on left.

1.9 ▲   SO FR 401.1 on left and closed track on right. Then intersection with FR 273.1 is on right and North-Central #27: Nevadaville Loop (FR 273.2) is on the left. Zero trip meter.

▼ 0.2   SO Intersection. North-Central #27: Nevadaville Loop (FR 739.1) on right. Follow FR 175.1 toward Columbine Campground.

1.7 ▲   SO Track on left is North-Central #27:

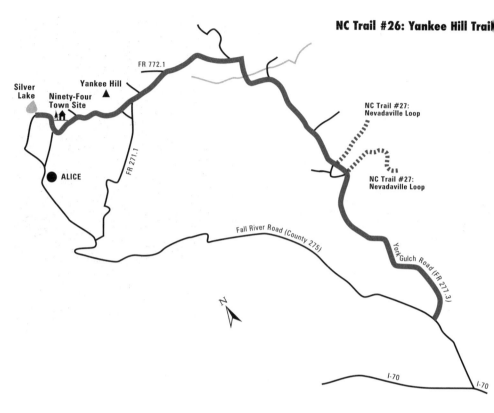

Nevadaville Loop (FR 739.1).

▼ 1.2	TL	Onto FR 175.2 toward St. Marys Glacier
0.7 ▲ TR		Onto FR 175.2.

▼ 1.9	BR	Intersection. Zero trip meter.
0.0 ▲		Continue along track.
		N 37°53.44' W 107°39.10'

▼ 0.0		Continue along FR 175.2.
4.3 ▲	BL	Intersection. Zero trip meter.

▼ 0.2	SO	Cross over creek.
4.1 ▲	SO	Cross over creek.

▼ 0.3	SO	Intersection. Track on right. Proceed straight ahead on FR 175.3B.
3.9	SO	Intersection. Track on left. Proceed straight ahead.

▼ 0.5	BL	Intersection with FR 175.3 on right. Straight ahead is FR 175.3C. Follow FR 175 sign, which is located about 75

yards past intersection.

3.7 ▲	BR	At intersection.
		N 39°49.72' W 105°35.27'

▼ 0.7	SO	Track enters on left.
3.6 ▲	BL	Track forks.

▼ 1.0	TL	Intersection. Follow FR 175.3.
3.3 ▲	TR	Intersection.
		N 39°49.85' W 105°35.72'

▼ 1.3	SO	Track on right.
2.9 ▲	SO	Track on left.

▼ 1.4	TL	Intersection. Road on right.
2.9 ▲	TR	Follow FR 175.3 sign.
		N 39°49.81' W 105°35.98'

▼ 1.5	BL	Intersection with FR 772.1 on right.
2.7 ▲	BR	FR 772.1 on left.

▼ 1.9	SO	FR 271.1F on left.
4.1 ▲	SO	FR 271.1F on right.

▼ 2.1 BL Intersection with FR 175.3D on right.
2.2 ▲ BR Intersection with FR 175.3D on left.
Remain on FR 175.3.

▼ 2.4 BL Follow FR 175.3 to the left. Track on right.
1.8 ▲ BR Follow FR 175.3.

▼ 2.6 BR Intersection on left is FR 271.1 to Cumberland Gulch and Fall River Road. Follow FR 175.4 toward St. Mary's Glacier.
1.7 ▲ BL Intersection with FR 271.1 on right goes through Cumberland Gulch.

▼ 2.6 SO Alternate route to FR 271.1 (Cumberland Gulch Road) on left.
1.6 ▲ BL Alternate route to FR 271.1 (Cumberland Gulch Road) on right.

▼ 3.0 SO Intersection with FR 271.1D. Follow FR 175.4.
1.2 SO Intersection with FR 271.1D. Follow FR 175.4.

▼ 3.2 SO Road enters on right.
1.1 ▲ BR Road forks.

▼ 3.2 BL Intersection. Remain on FR 175.4.
1.0 ▲ BR Intersection. Remain on FR 175.4.

▼ 3.6 SO Tailings dump on left.
0.7 ▲ SO Tailings dump on right.
N 39°49.62′ W 105°38.05′

▼ 3.7 SO Intersection with dead-end road on right; Ninety-Four town site.
0.6 ▲ SO Ninety-Four town site and intersection with dead-end road on left.

▼ 3.7 TR Intersection. Left goes to Alice.
0.5 ▲ TL Turn onto FR 175.4.
N 39°49.58′ W 105°38.21′

▼ 3.9 SO Crest Drive on left. Remain on Mine Road.
0.3 ▲ SO Crest Drive on right, then lodge.

▼ 4.1 TL Intersection at old mine.
0.2 ▲ TR At old mine.

▼ 4.2 TR Silver Lake.
0.1 ▲ TL Turn left after passing the lake.

▼ 4.2 End at the far side of Silver Lake, opposite Silver Lake Condos on left.
0.1 ▲ At the base of Silver Lake (about 8.7 miles along Fall River Road/County 275 from I-70), zero trip meter at the Silver Lake sign and proceed straight ahead.
N 39°49.80′ W 105°38.37′

Nevadaville Loop

STARTING POINT Central City
FINISHING POINT Central City
TOTAL MILEAGE 8.2 miles
UNPAVED MILEAGE 7.7 miles
DRIVING TIME 30 minutes
ROUTE ELEVATION 8,600 feet to 9,500 feet
USUALLY OPEN June to October
DIFFICULTY RATING 3
SCENIC RATING 8

Special Attractions

- Historic mining district.
- Central City and Nevadaville ghost town.

History

Gold was discovered in Gregory Gulch on May 6, 1859, and within weeks the area was teeming with thousands of prospectors. Newspaperman Horace Greeley rushed to the area to witness the scene and widely reported the find, attracting people from all over the world. Mountain City was the name of the first settlement in the area, but Central City soon absorbed it and became the dominant town.

Nevadaville, which was established at the same time as Central City, was also known as Nevada and Nevada City. The post office was established using the name Nevada but to avoid confusion with the California town, the name was changed to Bald Mountain. Although the post office used this name

CENTRAL CITY

From the initial gold discovery in 1859, Central City went from strength to strength. With the establishment of the Colorado Territory in 1861, the town graduated to become the Gilpin County seat. The boom caught the attention of financiers in the East, and Wall Street capital poured in to enable the rapid development of the mining district.

Central City was remarkable among mining towns in that it developed peaceably; the miners were unusually law abiding. By 1863, few people wore guns, and records of the next ten years, show that only sixteen men were killed in gunfights and brawls. In fact, in the only recorded gunfight, the participants fired at each other until their six-guns were empty, but not one shot hit its target.

An exception to this tranquility involved George Harrison, who owned the National Theater. In 1862, he had an argument with a local prizefighter named Charlie Switz. After a trip back East, Harrison returned with a group of actors and a new show for his theater. Upon hearing of his return, Switz realized that the time was ripe for him to finish their argument for once and all. He strapped on his guns and headed toward the stage depot. Harrison had been warned of the reception that awaited him and slipped off the stage as it drove into town. On spotting the heavily armed Switz, Harrison preemptively took aim and fired, killing him. By one account, he fired thirty-four more shots into Switz to make certain of the outcome. Harrison was arrested and tried for murder. His stated reason for the shooting was that he just plain didn't like Switz. The jury presumably felt that was good enough; they acquitted him.

Generally though, cultural pursuits seem to have been more to the liking of this mining community. The first theater in the city (which was then known as Mountain City) was the Montana. After it burned down, the Belvedere Theater was opened; productions there played to full houses. In 1878, the Central City Opera opened; Edwin Booth, Buffalo Bill, and Oscar Wilde were among the eclectic mix of famous performers to appear over the years. The Opera House became known as the best west of the Mississippi. It remains active today.

The lavish hotel named the Teller House was opened by mining and railroad man Henry M. Teller in June 1872. In 1934, on the floor in the bar, Herndon Davis, a Denver artist and newspaperman, painted the famous "Face on the Barroom Floor." After Colorado achieved statehood, Henry Teller served in the U.S. Senate for twenty-nine years.

At 10:00 a.m. on May 21, 1874, a fire started in the Chinatown section near the main business district and burned all day, destroying nearly the whole downtown, including the Montana Theater. Only six buildings remained, one being the brick Teller House. The town rallied, and brick and stone construction soon replaced what had been lost.

Two stages daily came to Central City from Denver and Georgetown. There were three schools, one of which had the first public school library in Colorado. A weekly newspaper started in 1862 and expanded to publish daily in 1876. By this time there were more than fifty businesses established in the town, including four firms of attorneys. Some may argue over whether the attorneys provided a less painful method of resolving disputes than gunfights, which were more usual in mining towns of the period.

Central City circa 1885

The town of Nevadaville today

until it closed in 1921, the residents continued to use Nevadaville.

Within its first year Nevadaville had grown to more than 2,000 residents, which made it larger than Denver. In 1860, the fledgling town passed a resolution that "there be no Bawdy houses, Grog Shops, or Gambling Saloons." However, this resolution was either overturned or not enforced because reports indicate that later there were thirteen saloons operating in the town. The biggest problem was lack of a reliable water supply. Ditches were dug from both Peck Gulch and Fall River but neither solved the shortage. The town suffered five devastating fires.

The Leadville boom in 1879 caused many residents to move on, and the town was nearly deserted in the wake of the 1893 silver panic. After the last fire in 1914, the town was not rebuilt. Nevadaville staged a few brief revivals, but by 1930 the population was two. Today, only a handful of structures remain.

Description

This is a reasonably simple loop to navigate with a number of side trails that can be explored. Mining activity abounds, especially from Central City until shortly past Nevadaville. The road is easy to Nevadaville; from there it gets a little rougher, but under dry conditions, it is not difficult at any point.

If you like learning history from headstones, this route provides many opportunities. Shortly past Nevadaville is the Bald Mountain Cemetery and toward the end of the route are four Central City cemeteries clustered around the intersection where the Boodle Mill is located.

Current Road Conditions

Arapaho and Roosevelt National Forest
Clear Creek Ranger District
101 Chicago Creek
Idaho Springs, CO 80452
(303) 567-3000

Nevadaville circa 1895

NC Trail #27: Nevadaville Loop

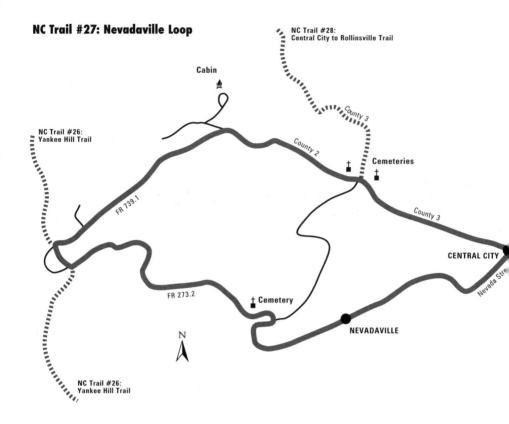

Map References

USFS   Arapaho and Roosevelt NF
USGS Gilpin County
Trails Illustrated, #103
The Roads of Colorado, p. 71
Colorado Atlas & Gazetteer, p. 39

Route Directions

▼ 0.0		Take Spring or Main Street to the intersection of Bridge and Nevada Streets. Zero trip meter and follow Nevada Street out of town to the southwest.
4.3 ▲		End at the intersection of Bridge and Nevada Streets in Central City.
		N 39°47.95′ W 105°30.73′

▼ 0.5	SO	Unpaved.
3.8 ▲	SO	Paved.

▼ 1.1	SO	Nevadaville.
3.2 ▲	SO	Nevadaville.

▼ 2.3	TL	Intersection. Turn onto FR 273.2.
2.0 ▲	TR	Onto road to Nevadaville.
		N 39°47.72′ W 105°32.54′

▼ 2.6	SO	Bald Mountain (Nevadaville) Cemetery on right.
1.7 ▲	SO	Bald Mountain (Nevadaville) Cemetery on left.

▼ 3.5	SO	Small track on left.
0.7 ▲	SO	Small track on right.

▼ 4.2	BL	Fork in road. FR 401.1 is to the right. Follow FR 273.2.
0.1 ▲	SO	FR 401.1 enters on left.
		N 39°48.10′ W 105°34.01′

▼ 4.3	TR	Track on left, then intersection with North-Central #26: Yankee Hill Trail. FR 277.3 is to the left and FR 175.1 is to the right. Zero trip meter.
0.0 ▲		Continue along FR 273.2 toward Nevadaville.

▼ 0.0   Continue along FR 175.1.

3.9 ▲   TL   Intersection with FR 273.2. North-Central #26: Yankee Hill Trail continues straight on. Zero trip meter.

▼ 0.2   TR   Intersection turn right onto FR 739.1 toward Central City. North-Central #26: Yankee Hill Trail continues straight on.

3.7 ▲   TL   Intersection with FR 175.1 (North-Central #26 Yankee Hill Trail).

     N 39°48.16' W 105°34.28'

▼ 0.3   BR   Fork in the road. Stay on FR 739.1.

3.6 ▲   BL   Intersection on right. Stay on FR 739.1

▼ 0.4   SO   Concrete foundation on left.

3.5 ▲   SO   Concrete foundation on right.

▼ 0.5   BR   Intersection with County 2. Columbine Campground is to the left.

3.4 ▲   BL   Onto FR 739.1.

     N 39°48.84' W 105°32.87'

▼ 2.6   SO   Cemetery on left.

1.3 ▲   SO   Cemetery on right.

▼ 2.7   SO   Intersection at Boodle Mill.

1.2 ▲   SO   Follow sign to Columbine Campground.

▼ 2.8   BR   Intersection with County 3. On the left is North-Central #28: Central City to Rollinsville Trail.

1.1 ▲   BL   Fork in road; proceed toward Columbine Campground. On the right is North-Central #28: Central City to Rollinsville Trail.

     N 39°48.48' W 105°31.78'

▼ 3.2   Paved.

0.7 ▲   Unpaved.

▼ 3.4   BR   Road becomes "H" Street, then Prosser.

0.5 ▲   SO   Road on left; follow Eureka Street

▼ 3.6   TR   Onto Eureka Street.

0.3 ▲   SO   Road on left, follow Eureka Street.

▼ 3.9   End at intersection with Main Street in Central City.

0.0 ▲   At the intersection of Main Street and Eureka Street in Central City, zero trip meter and proceed northwest out of town on Eureka.

     N 39°48.05' W 105°30.75'

Central City to Rollinsville Trail

STARTING POINT County 3 and County 2, 1.1 miles northwest of Central City

FINISHING POINT Colorado 119 in Rollinsville, approximately 13 miles north of Black Hawk

TOTAL MILEAGE 16.2 miles

UNPAVED MILEAGE 15.4 miles

DRIVING TIME 1 hour

ROUTE ELEVATION 8,600 feet to 10,600 feet

USUALLY OPEN June to October

DIFFICULTY RATING 3

SCENIC RATING 8

Special Attractions

■ Historic mining area.

■ Access to a network of 4WD roads.

History

This trail passes the sites of a number of old mining towns. Apex, founded in 1891 and platted in 1895, was established to provide housing for the miners working the several good mines within a mile of town. The town reached its peak population around 1896. It had two hotels, a dance hall, several churches, a school, and a newspaper called *The Apex Pine Cone*. The post office opened in 1894 and closed in 1932.

The most productive mine was the Mackey, named for its original owner. After it changed hands a number of times, it came under the ownership of a man by the name of Mountz, who formed a partnership to

Apex in 1890

until 1944. The railroad relocated a large brick station from Denver and rebuilt it at Tolland. This substantial structure with its large, covered platform had lunch rooms and a souvenir shop for the thousands of tourists that used to make the journey from Denver to fish, hike, picnic, or just admire the summer wildflowers.

Rollinsville was established by General John Q. Rollins, a prominent man who had many interests in mining, cattle ranching, and hotels throughout the Midwest and Rocky Mountains. Rollins improved the old army road that crossed Rollins Pass, then called Boulder Pass. Before the army arrived, the route had been a favorite Indian trail and is also believed to have been the route taken by the Mormons on their way to Salt Lake City.

Rollins obtained a charter in 1866 to build a freight road over the pass as a toll road. The road opened in 1873, and to service the captive audience using his toll road, he built the town of Rollinsville, which included a large hotel that he named the Rollins House. He also owned

develop it. After $30,000 worth of ore had been shipped, the partner stole all but $400 and disappeared. Convinced that there was a rich vein to be found, Mountz continued to operate the mine, but soon exhausted his funds. Out of frustration, he set a charge with the last of his dynamite to collapse the mine. With this last desperate act, he uncovered the elusive main vein of ore. It was assayed at $1,800 per ton; he had finally struck it rich.

Nugget was a one-mine camp that thrived in the late 1890s. A post office was opened in 1895 but closed only six years later. The town soon faded because of its proximity to American City, only half a mile north. There was not enough activity to support both towns, and American City proved to be the more successful.

Tolland, first called Mammoth, was originally a mining town but became a stage way station between Rollinsville and Middle Park. In 1904, when the railroad came through on its way to Rollins Pass before the nearby Moffat Tunnel opened, the town became a railroad station. A post office opened at this time and remained in operation

Rollinsville circa 1920

he local stagecoach service and the lumber operation. When establishing the own, he outlawed saloons, dance halls, rostitution, and gambling. Rollins also perated a number of nearby mines and e built a mill near the town to process he ore. However, even in the town's heyay, the population never exceeded 200. s the importance of the pass road and he mines waned, saloons were allowed to pen in the town but Rollins continued to ecline.

escription

he road to Apex is a maintained county oad through pleasant ranch land. From the own of Apex, the road gets bumpy but is till easy.

There is a great deal of historic mining ctivity still evident until the road passes he Nugget town site. From the ridge past he Elk Park area there are good views to he southwest to Kingston Peak and the urrounding area, and northwest to the Rollins Pass area. As you continue toward olland, there are also good views ahead to outh Boulder Creek Valley and, in the all, across large stands of wonderful goldn aspens.

The most difficult section of road is the tretch between Nugget and Tolland. It can e rough and rutted, especially late in the eason. Nonetheless, it remains relatively asy and from the intersection with County 6 (Rollins Pass Road); the road is maintained by the county.

urrent Road Conditions

Arapaho and Roosevelt National Forest
Clear Creek Ranger District
01 Chicago Creek
daho Springs, CO 80452
303) 567-3000

Map References

USFS Arapaho and Roosevelt NF
USGS Gilpin County
Trails Illustrated, #103
The Roads of Colorado, p. 71
Colorado Atlas & Gazetteer, p. 39

Route Directions

▼ 0.0   Begin at the intersection of County 3 and Columbine Campground Road (CC 2), 1.1 miles northwest of Central City via Eureka Street. Zero trip meter and continue northwest along County 3.

5.3 ▲   End at the intersection of County 3 and Columbine Campground Road (CC 2), 1.1 miles northwest of Central City.
N 39°48.48′ W 105°31.78′

▼ 0.1   SO   Cemetery grounds on left; Central City Cemetery on right.
5.2 ▲   SO   Cemeteries on left and right.

▼ 0.9   SO   Chase Gulch Reservoir on right.
4.4 ▲   SO   Chase Gulch Reservoir on left.

▼ 2.3   TL   Bridge over Clear Creek, then intersection. Turn onto County 4 S.
3.1 ▲   TR   Onto Central City 3.
N 39°49.81′ W 105°33.16′

▼ 5.3   TL   Town of Apex. Turn onto Apex Road (County 4 N) and zero trip meter.
0.0 ▲   Continue along County 4 S.
N 39°51.93′ W 105°34.16′

▼ 0.0   Continue along Apex Road.
10.7 ▲   TR   At town of Apex, turn onto County 4 S.

▼ 0.7   SO   Track on right.
10.0 ▲   SO   Track on left.

▼ 1.2   SO   Town site of Nugget. Cross through Elk Creek. Although there are a number of side roads, remain on main track.
9.5 ▲   SO   Town site of Nugget.
N 39°51.96′ W 105°35.46′

▼ 1.7   SO   Faint track on right.
8.9 ▲   SO   Faint track on left.

▼ 2.0   SO   Faint tracks on left and right.
8.7 ▲   SO   Faint tracks on left and right.

▼ 2.1   SO   Enter Roosevelt National Forest and cross cattle guard. Then tracks on left.
8.6 ▲   SO   Tracks on right. Cross cattle guard and

NC Trail #28: Central City to Rollinsville Trail

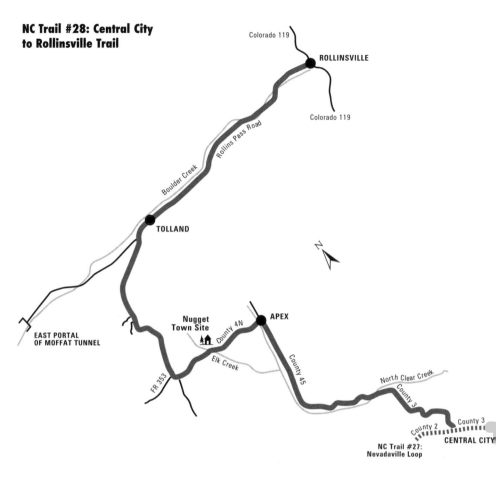

	leave Roosevelt National Forest.	5.0 ▲ TL Onto FR 176 (County 4 N) toward Apex.
▼ 2.2	TR Intersection. FR 353 goes to the left. Follow sign to Rollinsville.	**N 39°54.25′ W 105°35.47′**
8.5 ▲	TL Turn toward Apex.	
	N 39°51.99′ W 105°38.56′	▼ 5.9 SO Town of Tolland.
		4.8 ▲ SO Town of Tolland.
▼ 3.4	SO Track on right. Follow sign to FR 176.	▼ 8.1 SO Picnic area on left.
7.2 ▲	SO Follow sign marked FR 353.	2.6 ▲ SO Picnic area on right.
▼ 4.0	SO Tracks on left to Mammoth Basin and Old Reservoir site. Continue toward Rollinsville.	▼ 10.7 End at intersection with Colorado 119 in Rollinsville, approximately 13 miles north of Black Hawk.
6.6 ▲	SO Tracks on right to Mammoth Basin and Old Reservoir site. Continue toward Apex.	0.0 ▲ From Colorado 119 in Rollinsville (just after bridge over railroad line if heading north), zero trip meter and turn onto FR 176 (County 16) toward the Moffat Tunnel.
▼ 5.6	TR Intersection with Rollins Pass Road. Moffat Tunnel is three miles to the left.	**N 39°55.03′ W 105°30.12′**

Selected Further Reading

Abbott, Carl, Stephen J. Leonard, and David McComb. *Colorado: A History of the Centennial State.* Niwot, Colo.: University Press of Colorado, 1994.

Aldrich, John K. *Ghosts of Clear Creek County.* Lakewood, Colo.: Centennial Graphics, 1992.

Aldrich, John K. *Ghosts of Gilpin County.* Lakewood, Colo.: Centennial Graphics, 1996.

Aldrich, John K. *Ghosts of Lake County.* Lakewood, Colo.: Centennial Graphics, 1997.

Aldrich, John K. *Ghosts of Park County.* Lakewood, Colo.: Centennial Graphics, 1994.

Aldrich, John K. *Ghosts of Summit County.* Lakewood, Colo.: Centennial Graphics, 1997.

Bancroft, Caroline. *Colorful Colorado.* Boulder, Colo.: Johnson Books, 1987.

Bancroft, Caroline. *Unique Ghost Towns and Mountain Spots.* Boulder, Colo.: Johnson Books, 1961.

Bauer, Carolyn. *Colorado Ghost Towns—Colorado Traveler Guidebooks.* Frederick, Colo.: Renaissance House, 1987.

Beckner, Raymond M. *Along the Colorado Rail.* Pueblo, Colo.: O'Brien Printing & Stationery, 1975.

Benham, Jack. *Ouray.* Ouray, Colo.: Bear Creek Publishing, 1976.

Boyd, Leanne C. and H. Glenn Carson.

Atlas of Colorado Ghost Towns. Vols. 1 and 2. Deming, N.M.: Carson Enterprises, Ltd., 1984.

Bright, William. *Colorado Place Names.* Boulder, Colo.: Johnson Books, 1993.

Brown, Robert L. *Colorado Ghost Towns Past & Present.* Caldwell, Idaho: Caxton Printers, Ltd., 1972.

Brown, Robert L. *Ghost Towns of the Colorado Rockies.* Caldwell, Idaho: Caxton Printers, Ltd., 1990.

Brown, Robert L. *Jeep Trails to Colorado Ghost Towns.* Caldwell, Idaho: Caxton Printers, Ltd., 1995.

Bueler, Gladys R. *Colorado's Colorful Characters.* Boulder, Colo.: Pruett Publishing, 1981.

Carver, Jack, Jerry Vondergeest, Dallas Boyd, and Tom Pade. *Land of Legend.* Denver, Colo.: Caravon Press, 1959.

Crofutt, George A. *Crofutt's Grip-Sack Guide of Colorado.* Omaha: Overland Publishing, 1885. Reprinted, Boulder, Colo.: Johnson Books, 1981.

Cromie, Alice. *A Tour Guide to the Old West.* Nashville, Tenn.: Rutledge Hill Press, 1990.

Crutchfield, James A. *It Happened in Colorado.* Helena & Billings, Mont.: Falcon Press Publishing, 1993.

Dallas, Sandra. *Colorado Ghost Towns and Mining Camps.* Norman, Okla.: University of Oklahoma Press, 1985.

DeLong, Brad. *4-Wheel Freedom.* Boulder,

Colo.: Paladin Press, 1996.

Dorset, Phyllis Flanders. *The New Eldorado: The Story of Colorado's Gold & Silver Rushes.* New York: Macmillan, 1970.

Eberhart, Perry. *Guide to the Colorado Ghost Towns and Mining Camps.* Chicago, Ill.: Swallow Press, 1995.

Fisher, Vardis, and Opal Laurel Holmes. *Gold Rushes and Mining Camps of the Early American West.* Caldwell, Idaho: Caxton Printers, Ltd., 1968.

Florin, Lambert. *Ghost Towns of the West.* New York: Promontory Press, 1993.

Foster, Mike. *Strange Genius: The Life of Ferdinand Vandeveer Hayden.* Niwot, Colo.: Roberts Rinehart Publishers, 1994.

Green, Stewart M. *Bureau of Land Management Back Country Byways.* Helena, Mont.: Falcon Press, 1995.

Gregory, Lee. *Colorado Scenic Guide: Northern Region.* Boulder, Colo.: Johnson Books, 1990.

Griffin, Wayne W. *Central Colorado 4-Wheeling Guidebook.* Aspen, Colo.: Who Press, 1994.

Heck, Larry E. *4-Wheel Drive Trails & Ghost Towns of Colorado.* Aurora, Colo.: Pass Patrol.

Helmuth, Ed and Gloria. *The Passes of Colorado.* Boulder, Colo.: Pruett Publishing, 1994.

Hilton, George W. *American Narrow Gauge Railroads.* Stanford: Stanford University Press.

Jessen, Ken. *Colorado Gunsmoke: True Stories of Outlaws and Lawmen on the Colorado Frontier.* Loveland, Colo.: J. V. Publications, 1986.

Koch, Don. *The Colorado Pass Book.* Boulder, Colo.: Pruett Publishing, 1992.

McLean, Evalyn Walsh. *Father Struck it Rich.* Fort Collins, Colo.: FirstLight, 1996.

McTighe, James. *Roadside History of Colorado.* Boulder, Colo.: Johnson Books, 1984.

Noel, Thomas J., Paul F. Mahoney, and Richard E. Stevens. *Historical Atlas of Colorado.* Norman, Okla.: University of Oklahoma Press, 1994.

Norton, Boyd and Barbara. *Backroads of Colorado.* Stillwater, Minn: Voyageur Press, 1995.

Ormes, Robert M. *Railroads and the Rockies.* Denver, Colo.: Sage Books, 1963.

Ormes, Robert. *Tracking Ghost Railroads in Colorado.* Colorado Springs, Colo.: Green Light Graphics, 1992.

Parker, Ben H., Jr. *Gold Panning and Placering in Colorado.* Denver, Colo.: U.S. Geological Survey, Department of Natural Resources, 1992.

Pettem, Silvia. *Colorado Mountains & Passes—Colorado Traveler Guidebooks.* Frederick, Colo.: Renaissance House, 1991.

Pettit, Jan. *Utes: The Mountain People.* Boulder, Colo.: Johnson Books, 1994.

Pritchard, Sandra F. *Men, Mining & Machines.* Dillon, Colo.: Summit County Historical Society, 1996.

Sagstetter, Beth and Bill. *The Mining Camps Speak.* Denver, Colo.: BenchMark Publishing of Colorado, 1998.

Sinnotte, Barbara. *Colorado: A Guide to the State & National Parks.* Edison, N.J.: Hunter, 1996.

Smith, Duane A. *Colorado Mining: A Photographic History.* Albuquerque, N.M.: University of New Mexico Press, 1977.

Southworth, Dave. *Colorado Mining Camps.* Wild Horse, 1997.

Southworth, Dave. *Gunfighters of the Old West.* Wild Horse, 1997.

Taylor, Colin F. *The Plains Indians.* New York: Barnes & Noble Books and Salamander Books, 1997.

Ubbelohde, Carl, Maxine Benson, and Duane A. Smith. *A Colorado History.* Boulder, Colo.: Pruett Publishing, 1995.

Von Bamford, Lawrence, and Kenneth R. Tremblay, Jr. Leadville Architecture. Estes Park, Colo.: Architecture Research Press,

996.

Waldman, Carl. *Encyclopedia of Native American Tribes.* New York: Facts on File, 1988.

Wilkins, Tivis E. *Colorado Railroads Chronological Development.* Boulder, Colo.: Pruett Publishing, 1974.

Wilson, Ray D. *Colorado Historical Tour Guide.* Carpentersville, Ill.: Crossroads Communications, 1990.

Wolle, Muriel Sibell. *The Bonanza Trail.* Chicago, Ill.: The Swallow Press, 1953.

Photographic Credits

About the Authors

Peter Massey grew up in the outback of Australia. After retiring from a career in investment banking at the age of thirty-five, he served as a director of a number of companies in the United States, the United Kingdom, and Australia. He moved to Colorado in 1993.

Jeanne Wilson was born and grew up in Washington, D.C. She lived and worked in New York City as a young adult and has been a resident of Colorado since 1993.

Traveling extensively in Australia, Europe, Asia, and Africa, the authors covered more than 80,000 miles touring throughout the United States and outback Australia in the past five years. They traveled more than 15,000 miles in Colorado to research their books.

The authors' first book, *4WD Adventures: Colorado,* is a compilation of more than 70 exciting and interesting trails in Colorado. The fully illustrated volume includes detailed information about Colorado towns, ghost towns, historical characters, wildlife, and wildflowers that relate to each route.

ORDER FORM

To purchase any of our Colorado Trails books, contact your local book or map store or order direct from Adler Publishing by any of the following methods:

Telephone orders: **800-660-5107**
Or fax your order: **310-698-0709**
Or order on-line: **4WDbooks.com**
Or mail your order to this address: **Adler Publishing Company, Inc.**
1601 Pacific Coast Highway, Suite 290
Hermoas Beach, CA 90254

- -

I understand that I may return any book for a full refund—for any reason, no questions asked.

	Price	Quantity	Total
Colorado Trails: North-Central	$16.95		
WD Trails: Southwest	$14.95		
Colorado Trails: South-Central	$16.95		
WD Adventures: Colorado	$29.95		

Shipping and handling $4 for the first book and $3 for each additional book. California residents add 8% sales tax and Colorado residents add 3% sales tax.

Sub Total _____
Tax _____
Shipping _____
Total _____

Send my order to:

NAME (PLEASE PRINT) _____

COMPANY _____

STREET ADDRESS _____

CITY / STATE / ZIP _____

TELEPHONE ( ) _____

Method of payment:

❑ Check or money order enclosed
❑ VISA   ❑ MasterCard   ❑ American Express

CARD NUMBER _____

EXPIRATION DATE _____

CARDHOLDER'S SIGNATURE _____